pand

Matthew Somerled Macdonald

Abstract

An instance of epistemically circular justification is one in which a justification source successfully justifies the claim that it is a justification source. It is generally thought that this is impossible. However, there is also reason to think that our fundamental evidential sources and theories of justification cannot be justified without circularity. In this thesis I investigate the problem of epistemic circularity in detail. First, I'll examine a prominent argument for thinking that the justification of our fundamental evidential sources must be circular, and show that it is not decisive. My response employs a pragmatic account of justification, whereby your goals and preferences can make you justified in believing something even when you lack evidence for it. Second, I'll offer a different argument for thinking that epistemically circular justification is possible.

Acknowledgements

I am indebted to many for help and encouragement during the course of writing this thesis. Foremost thanks I owe to my supervisors Professor Simon Keller and Professor Edwin Mares for invaluable discussion, feedback and support. I have also benefited greatly from financial help in the form of a Victoria Master's Scholarship.

I owe a hefty debt of gratitude to the Victoria philosophy staff and postgraduate community for providing a friendly and supportive environment throughout the course of my studies, and especially to Matthew O'Leary, Josef Holden and Toby Vandenberg for useful discussion in developing my views.

In addition, I would like to thank audiences at the 2014 Australasian Postgraduate Philosophy Conference and the 2014 New Zealand Association of Philosophy Conference, as well as audiences at Victoria University's weekly postgraduate philosophy seminar series and the 2014 Postgraduate Philosophy Retreat.

Lastly, I owe special thanks to Erika Webb for her support and encouragement during the course of writing this thesis.

Table of Contents

Introduction

An instance of epistemic circularity occurs when your justification for thinking that something is a justification source comes from that source. For example, suppose I try to convince you that the testimony of a particular mystic guru provides justification. The reason why that claim is justified (I might argue) is that the guru himself said it; and since his testimony provides justification, the claim is justified! Suppose also that I rely on no other evidence. It is not as if I am testing what he says against an independent source. I am relying on the guru's testimony to justify the claim that it is a source of justification.

This kind of reasoning looks very suspicious. It is odd to think that we could gain justification to trust the guru simply by trusting him. In fact, it seems that there is something impermissible in general about trusting a source to prove its own justificatory efficacy. One reason is that epistemically circular arguments are dialectically ineffective. When I try to persuade you that the guru's testimony provides justification by appealing to what he says, you should find my argument unpersuasive. If you don't already believe me, you will have no reason to accept my evidence; and if you do already believe me, you simply won't require it. So it seems like there is no good reason to accept an argument which relies on the source it tries to justify.

Sources which purport to justify their own efficacy also keep bad company. If justification could be provided in a circular fashion, it looks like all kinds of dodgy evidential sources could justify themselves. But we shouldn't want the guru to prove that his testimony provides justification simply by saying so! If we allow that circular justification is possible, we risk making it too easy to justify evidential sources whose efficacy should be a lot harder to vindicate.

The 'bad company' problem also affects rules of inference. If it is possible to use a rule to show that the rule transmits justification from premises to a conclusion, then it is easy to show that certain bogus forms of reasoning can do the same. Consider the gambler's fallacy for example. This involves inferring, from the observation that things of a particular kind have lacked a particular property, that future observations of that kind are more likely to have that property.

The gambler's fallacy is sometimes applied in roulette. A roulette ball will typically fall into either a red or a black pocket on each spin, and it can be tempting to infer from a run of blacks (for instance) that the likelihood of red on the next spin will be greater. In fact, the rule is faulty: the ball is no more or less likely to land in red given that it landed in black last time than it would be otherwise. Indeed, millions of francs were lost in Monte Carlo Casino one day in 1913 when a roulette ball landed black 26 times in a row, by gamblers who applied this kind of bad reasoning.[1]

But if epistemically circular justification is possible, we can use the gambler's fallacy to show that such inferences actually work. After all, reasoning in accordance with the gambler's fallacy has typically failed dismally. So according to the rule itself, future instances of it are very likely to succeed![2]

The dialectical ineffectiveness problem and the bad company problem are reasons to be suspicious of epistemic circularity.[3] Circular reasoning seems irresponsible and illegitimate. It does not seem like the kind of reasoning we want to allow, and an epistemology that does allow it seems all the worse. So it is tempting to say that no source can ever justify the claim that it is a source of justification.

---

[1] Haunsperger & Kennedy (2007).
[2] Rosen (2009, pg. 157).
[3] See Boghossian (2000, 2001) for further discussion of these two problems.

However, instituting a ban on epistemic circularity is more difficult than it seems. This is because it is hard to show that our most basic sources of evidence and rules of inference can provide justification without relying on the sources and rules themselves.

Take an evidential source like vision, for instance. This is a basic and fundamental evidential source, in the sense that much of what we believe about the outside world is ultimately acquired through the use of it, and in the sense that many of these beliefs would be compromised if we found that it did not reflect the way things are.

Of course, we do think that vision reliably reflects the world. And the natural way of justifying this claim is to appeal to what we scientifically know about vision. We can, for instance, provide a proximal explanation about how the eye and the visual cortex work, which explains why visual perception is reasonably accurate. And we can also give a distal explanation about how creatures like us evolved to have good vision in response to certain selection pressures over the course of our evolutionary history.

The problem is that the evidence on which those explanations are based could only have been acquired by using visual perception. Our understanding of the eye and visual cortex is built up from a large number of observations, including observations made by the use of microscopes and other instruments, but the ultimate means by which we access that evidence is through vision. And our understanding of evolution is based on a large number of observations about the biology and genetics of different organisms, as well as about the history of their development. Ultimately, that evidence was acquired by visual perception as well. So giving a scientific explanation for why vision is reliable amounts to establishing the justificatory efficacy of vision by trusting it.[4]

[4] See Alston (1986) for discussion of the circular justification of visual perception.

Could we justify vision by using a different evidential source? Even if we could, we face circularity. The justification of vision by a different source will only work if the efficacy of that source can also be established. Obviously, trusting the source to justify its own efficacy will be circular. And justifying it by trusting vision will ultimately just count as using vision to justify vision. So the only way of justifying an evidential source without falling into circularity is to keep appealing to new evidential sources.

Sooner or later though, we will run out. We have only a finite number of fundamental evidential sources, and if it's necessary to justify all of them, the commitment to circularity seems unavoidable. Sooner or later we will find that there is an evidential source which justifies its own efficacy – either directly, or in virtue of its being justified by a source whose own efficacy it supports. So it seems that ultimately, some evidential source can justify the claim that it is a source of justification.[5]

Epistemic circularity is also difficult to avoid in the justification of our most fundamental rules of inference. Consider the rule of induction. This involves inferring, from the observation that things of a particular kind have had a particular property, that future observations of that kind are also likely to have the property.

Unlike the gambler's fallacy, induction is quite a reliable rule of inference. But as David Hume (1739-40) pointed out, the most natural means of justifying this claim works out to be circular. It involves thinking that induction is likely to keep working in new cases, because previous instances of induction have typically been successful. This amounts to trusting induction in the course of establishing its own justificatory efficacy.[6]

---

[5] See Alexander (2011); Bergmann (2000) pg. 177-179.

[6] Hume also considers justifying induction deductively, and finds that this doesn't work. See Hume (1739-40:1978, 1:3:6, pp. 89-91; 1:3:8, pp. 104-105; 1:3:12, pp.130-142).

What I think we have here is an epistemological puzzle. On the one hand, epistemic circularity looks problematic. Just like giving an argument which features its conclusion as a premise, using a source to establish its own justificatory efficacy does not seem like the kind of thing that should be allowed. Not only are circular arguments unpersuasive, but to allow circular justification is to risk allowing all kinds of dodgy sources to justify themselves. However, it is very difficult to avoid circularity in the justification of even ordinary, respectable sources of evidence and rules of inference. So epistemic circularity looks problematic, but necessary. As Baron Reed puts it:

> Epistemic circularity is inescapable. If it really is as bad as it seems, then scepticism is correct: our epistemic positions are fatally compromised.
> [Reed 2006, pg. 187]

In this thesis, I will examine whether legitimate instances of epistemically circular justification are possible. My view is that they are possible, but not for the reasons that have typically been thought.

In Chapter One, I will outline the major extant argument for thinking that legitimate circular justification is possible, which develops some of the concerns I raised earlier about the status of our evidential sources. Accordingly, we can call it the Argument from Evidential Circularity.

In Chapter Two, I will consider the prospects for developing a response to this argument which appeals to pragmatism about justification. This is the view that your goals and preferences can sometimes make you justified in believing a claim, even when you lack evidence for it. An existing version of this approach has been developed by Byeong Lee (2013). Although I think Lee's general strategy is promising, I will argue that his particular version of it fails.

In Chapter Three, I'll consider how we might improve on Lee's proposal. I'll look at two possible approaches, one of which is externalist in character and one of which is internalist. My view is that we ought not to ignore the demand for internally-accessible justification, and so I will endorse an internalist modification to Lee's original account. The modifications I propose trade on a broadly Humean view about the rational status of our preferences, as well as a fairly traditional view about our introspective access to our mental states.

In Chapter Four I will present a novel problem for pragmatism about justification, which threatens the plausibility of a pragmatic response to the Argument from Evidential Circularity. In order to avoid this problem, I will make an important modification to the basic pragmatist theory.

Lastly, in Chapter Five I will present a brand new argument for thinking that epistemically circular justification is possible. Although I hope to show that the Argument from Evidential Circularity is not decisive, I think my new argument is. So I will conclude that epistemically circular justification is possible for reasons other than those that have typically been offered.

In many places throughout this thesis I will formulate various epistemic principles and definitions, and I will present certain arguments in standard form. For ease of reference, I have reproduced all of these in two Appendices. Appendix A contains the principles and definitions, and Appendix B contains the arguments.

Chapter One: The Argument from Evidential Circularity

This Chapter discusses the major extant argument for thinking that epistemically circular justification is possible. It is divided into four sections. Section 1.1 will focus the discussion by providing a more detailed account of what epistemic circularity involves. Then, Section 1.2 will introduce the principle that in order to gain justification from a source of evidence, you need to have justification for thinking it reliable. The aim of the Section is to show that affirming the principle commits you to the claim that epistemically circular justification is possible. Section 1.3 will consider theories that deny this principle, and will show that a commitment to circular justification also follows from its denial. So the conclusion of the Argument from Evidential Circularity is that epistemically circular justification is possible unconditionally. Section 1.4 will consider the implications of this conclusion and our prospects for avoiding it.

1.1 What is Epistemic Circularity?[7]

Let's focus the discussion by refining our notion of epistemically circular justification. I will start by offering my own definition and explaining three of its main features. This will allow me to extend the definition to other epistemically relevant properties like knowledge and warrant. Although my main focus in this thesis will be on circular justification, I think the underlying structure is a general one, affecting any epistemically valuable property (and I will briefly consider epistemically circular properties besides justification in Section 5.2).

[7] The term 'epistemic circularity' was introduced by Alston (1986, pg. 10).

My definition of epistemically circular justification is as follows:

> [EC-J]: An instance of epistemically circular justification is one in which a justification source S provides you with justification for the claim 'S is a justification source'.

Let me explain this definition. First, it is important to differentiate epistemic circularity from logical circularity. Logical circularity is a property of arguments whereby the conclusion of the argument features amongst its premises. All logically circular arguments are valid – since the conclusion is also a premise, it is impossible for the premises to be true and the conclusion false. But logical circularity prevents an argument from transmitting new justification to its conclusion, because the conclusion must *already* be justified in order for the premises to be.

Epistemically circular arguments can be subtler. When I try to use the gambler's fallacy to show that it provides justification, I don't necessarily include my conclusion as a premise. Rather, I treat the gambler's fallacy as the inferential rule whereby I get from the evidence that it has typically failed to the conclusion that it will succeed. Similarly, when I try to establish that the guru's testimony provides justification by trusting him, I might not necessarily use my conclusion as a premise. It would be enough simply for me to treat the guru as the source of the evidence by which I establish that conclusion. So it isn't necessary that an argument includes its conclusion as a premise in order for it to count as epistemically circular.

Of course, it is standard to think about circularity as a property of arguments or chains of inference. But the notion I want to capture is broader. As I define it, epistemic circularity is really a property of instances of justification. And instances of justification are not necessarily inferential.

The concept of non-inferential justification should be familiar from theories such as process reliabilism (see Goldman, 1979; 2008). According to process reliabilism about justification, it is the fact that a belief is reliably caused which provides it with justification, not the fact that it is inferred from other beliefs. That is, your visual belief 'there is text in front of me' will be justified as long as your vision reliably reflects the world, even if you don't support your visual belief by inference. Of course, reliabilists don't *rule out* the idea that inference from other beliefs can provide justification (as long as the inferential practice is reliable), but the important thing about their position is that justification isn't *necessarily* inferential. And non-inferential justification is a feature of other theories as well.

An instance of non-inferential epistemically circular justification might look like the following. Suppose I believe that 'for any claim P, the fact that I believe P is a source of justification for P'. And suppose it were also true! Then, the claim itself would be justified in virtue of my believing it. So my act of believing would justify the claim that my act of believing is a source of justification. Then we would have an instance of epistemically circular justification, but the justification would not be inferential. So it isn't the case that epistemically circular justification is necessarily inferential.

Epistemic circularity should really be regarded as a property of instances of justification rather than of inferences. Instances of justification are just those sets of epistemically relevant facts that make it the case that a claim is justified. Of course, depending on whatever theory of justification is correct, it could turn out that non-inferential justification is impossible. But we can understand epistemic circularity without having to assume this from the outset. So this is a second way in which epistemic circularity differs from logical circularity.

We should also keep in mind the standard distinction between propositional and doxastic justification. Propositional justification is the kind of justification you can have for a claim whether or not you believe it. This might involve having sufficient evidence for that claim. For instance, you probably have sufficient evidence for the claim 'Wellington is further south than Damascus', even if you haven't explicitly considered it. So you have propositional justification. Once you believe it you gain doxastic justification. To have doxastic justification for a claim is to have propositional justification for it, and to believe it.

There is no reason to restrict epistemic circularity to doxastic justification. Just as it makes sense to have justification for a claim that you don't yet believe, it makes sense that your justification could be circular. If the guru's testimony really does justify the claim that it is a source of justification, and you know that he has made this claim, then you have epistemically circular propositional justification for it, whether or not you actually believe him.

I have presented my own definition of epistemically circular justification and explained three of its main features. An instance of epistemically circular justification is one in which a justification source S provides you with justification for the claim 'S is a justification source'. This can differ from logical circularity, since it doesn't require including the conclusion as the premise in an argument. And although epistemic circularity can be a property of arguments, it can also be a property of non-inferential justificatory structures as well. Lastly, epistemically circular justification can be propositional and not just doxastic. It can affect the justification of claims you don't yet believe.

I should point out that there have been other attempts to characterise epistemic circularity as well – most recently by Jesper Kallestrup (2012), who defines it as a property of arguments. I see no reason to restrict epistemic circularity to arguments, so my notion of circularity is broader than Kallestrup's. However I don't really intend my own definition to be a competing account. I've merely tried to pick out a pattern of justification which I think requires investigation, because it suffers from the problems I discussed in the Introduction.

I also think the pattern I have identified is a general one, affecting a variety of other epistemically valuable properties besides justification. That is, it also makes sense to consider epistemically circular knowledge, or warrant, or rational acceptability, and possibly other properties as well. For this reason, I would like to supplement my definition of circular justification with the following more general one:

> [EC-ε]: For any epistemically valuable property ε, an instance of epistemically circular ε is one in which an ε-source S provides you with ε for the claim 'S is an ε-source'.

So the definition of epistemically circular justification I formulated in [EC-J] is simply the instantiation of a more general pattern by which the source of an epistemically valuable property confers the property upon the claim that it is such a source. For example, an instance of circular knowledge is one in which your knowledge that something is a source of knowledge comes from that source. And an instance of circular warrant is one in which your warrant for thinking that a particular source provides warrant comes from that source. So questions about circular justification are just a subset of a broader set of questions about epistemic circularity.

The extent to which properties like justification, knowledge and warrant overlap is not something I will address. My thesis will focus predominantly on epistemically circular justification, though in Section 5.2 I will say a little about the circular provision of other properties. In addition, because the underlying structure of the problem is general, there are places later in the thesis where I draw on authors who focus on other properties, like knowledge. This should not detract from the relevance of their views to the problem of epistemically circular justification as well.

It is controversial whether genuine instances of epistemically circular justification are possible. In the remainder of this Chapter, I will introduce the Argument from Evidential Circularity for this claim. In Chapters Two, Three, and Four I will develop a response to it, and in Chapter Five I will offer a brand new argument for thinking that epistemically circular justification is possible.

1.2 The Problem of the Criterion

The Argument from Evidential Circularity is the main extant argument for thinking that epistemically circular justification is possible. It concerns the following principle for justification (adapted from Cohen 2002; 2010):

> [JR]: For any evidential source S, S provides you with justification only if you have justification for the claim 'S is reliable'.

The argument is an attempt to show that a commitment to the possibility of epistemically circular justification follows from the affirmation of this principle, and also from its denial. Since the principle is of course either true or false, the conclusion is that epistemically circular justification is possible unconditionally.

The reason for thinking that the affirmation of [JR] commits you to circularity is a version of the ancient Problem of the Criterion, originally developed by Pyrrhonian sceptics.[8] The idea is that your justification for thinking an evidential source reliable starts you off on an infinite regress which can only be terminated by a source that supports its own reliability. That amounts to the source providing justification for the claim that it is a source of justification, which is an instance of epistemic circularity. I will explain the Problem of the Criterion further in the course of this Section.

The reason for thinking that the denial of [JR] commits you to circularity comes from a problem known as the 'Bootstrapping Problem'. This was developed by Alston (1986), Fumerton (1995) and Vogel (2000). The idea is that any source which can provide you with justification in the absence of justification to think it reliable can quickly furnish you with evidence that it is reliable anyway. This allows you to use the source to show that it is a source of justification, which is an instance of epistemic circularity. I will explain the Bootstrapping Problem in Section 1.3.

The Argument from Evidential Circularity has been discussed in various different forms in a number of places. The Problem of the Criterion and the Bootstrapping Problem have been treated as separate arguments for the existence of circular justification, by philosophers who already commit themselves to the affirmation or to the denial of [JR] (e.g. Van Cleve 2003, Alexander 2011, Bergmann 2000). They have also been used as reasons to reject particular theories which affirm or deny [JR] on the grounds that circular justification is impossible (e.g. Vogel 2000, Fumerton 1995). But some authors (such as Alston 1986; Cohen 2002, 2005, 2010; Zalabardo 2005) do explicitly address the Argument from Evidential Circularity in its entirety.

---

[8] Sextus Empiricus. *Outlines of Pyrrhonism*. Book II. Trans. Bury, R. (1990). See also Chisholm (1973).

Considering the Problem of the Criterion and the Bootstrapping Problem together in the course of a single argument reveals that epistemic circularity is a deep problem, affecting a variety of theories. Since [JR] is either true or false, the commitment to circularity should represent a challenge to any view of justification. It's not possible to use the Problem of the Criterion or the Bootstrapping Problem (together with the claim that circular justification is impossible) as grounds to reject a rival theory unless it can be shown that one of the Problems is not genuine.

Let us go over the Argument from Evidential Circularity in detail before considering its implications and some possible responses. We will start by looking at the Problem of the Criterion, which arises if we affirm [JR]. The formulation I present is my own, though it draws on formulations by Alexander (2011) and Bergmann (2000).

Accordingly, let us assume for the sake of argument that [JR] is correct:

1. [JR]: For any evidential source S, S provides you with justification only if you have justification for the claim 'S is reliable'. [Assumed]

Of course, there wouldn't be much use in affirming [JR] unless we also thought that some evidential sources actually do provide us with justification. Obviously this will beg the question against the sceptic who thinks that no evidential sources provide justification at all. But the Argument from Evidential Circularity isn't a response to the sceptic, it is an attempt to show that ordinary non-sceptics are committed to the possibility of epistemically circular justification. Accordingly, we can assert that:

2. There is an evidential source S^1 which provides you with justification. [Premise]

3. ∴ You have justification for the claim 'S^1 is reliable'. [1, 2]

To say that an evidential source is reliable is just to say that it tends to accurately reflect the world. This is not just a claim about its previous record: it is a modal claim about how we can expect the source to perform in a variety of ordinary circumstances (see Alston 1986, pg. 2). Of course, the source doesn't have to perform perfectly in every case. But it does have to reflect the world reasonably often and reasonably well in order for it to count as reliable.

Our fundamental sources of evidence about the world are faculties like vision, hearing, touch, and memory. Our evidence is ultimately acquired through these faculties. But the reliability of our fundamental evidential sources isn't guaranteed. To say that vision is reliable, for instance, is to make a general, contingent and fallible claim about the world. It is very difficult to see how a claim like that can be justified *a priori*.

The kinds of claims that are typically thought to be justified *a priori* include analytic claims, which are true just in virtue of the meanings of the words. For instance, it is analytic that 'all bachelors are unmarried males.' And they include the necessary truths of logic and mathematics, such as '1+1=2.' They also include a special class of self-evident contingent claims, such as 'I am thinking now.' Self-evident claims can be justified *a priori,* because the occurrence of beliefs affirming them count as sufficient evidence for their content. Although it isn't a necessary truth that 'I am thinking now', the claim is made true whenever I believe it, so it counts as justified *a priori*.

Many epistemologists writing on circularity have found it implausible that the reliability of our fundamental evidential sources can be justified *a priori*. For instance, James Van Cleve (2003) writes that:

> Principles affirming the reliability of our faculties are both *contingent* and *general*. For me, it is hard to see how a principle combining these features can be basic – at least if basic propositions comprise only those that are somehow immediately evident or obvious. [Van Cleve 2003, pg. 51]

William Alston (1986) agrees:

> What alternatives are there to justification by adequate reasons? Even if we are justified in accepting propositions that seem self-evident to us, that would not seem to apply here. Any tendency to suppose [the reliability of our evidential sources] to be self-evident can be put down to a confusion between self-evidence and being strongly inclined to accept the proposition without question. [Alston 1986, pg. 4]

Stewart Cohen (2002) expresses suspicion:

> The reliability of our cognitive processes is a contingent matter. And so to know *a priori* that they are reliable would be to have contingent *a priori* knowledge. Surely this should give us pause. [Cohen 2002, pg. 320][9,10]

Byeong Lee (2013) is more forthright:

> Note that ['our perceptual judgements are generally reliable'] is a fallible claim with substantial empirical content. In order to establish the correctness of [that claim], we need to establish that most of our perceptual judgments have been true. [Lee 2013, pg. 2]

---

[9] Cohen is more sympathetic to contingent *a priori* knowledge in his (2010). But even there he admits that it 'has the air of "pulling the rabbit out of the hat".' (pg. 156).

[10] Cohen talks about knowledge rather than justification – see my qualification at the end of Section 1.1.

The sentiment these philosophers express seems plausible, at least at the outset. It doesn't look like we can have justification for thinking our sources reliable unless we get that justification from evidence. Accordingly:

4. For any evidential source S, justification for the claim 'S is reliable' can only come from an evidential source. [Premise]

In addition, the relation of justification between evidential sources is transitive. This means that whenever source A justifies a claim affirming the reliability of source B, and source B justifies the reliability of source C, the reliability of C is ultimately justified by source A – as long as we lack independent justification for thinking C reliable. This is revealed by the observation that, were we to doubt the reliability of A, we would have reason to doubt the reliability of C. Hence:

5. For any evidential sources S^A, S^B and S^C, if your justification for the claim 'S^C is reliable' comes from S^B, and your justification for the claim 'S^B is reliable' comes from S^A, then your justification for the claim 'S^C is reliable' ultimately comes from S^A. [Premise]

Moreover, the number of our fundamental evidential sources is finite. When we examine where our evidence about the world comes from, we find that our evidential sources ultimately resolve themselves into a small set of sensory and similar capacities through which all of our other evidence is acquired. Exactly how we individuate and characterise these capacities isn't the main focus here. For the purposes of the argument, it is enough to say that:

6. You have only a finite number of evidential sources. [Premise]

The result is that your justification for thinking S^1 reliable will ultimately come from an evidential source S^N. Because S^1 can provide you with justification, it follows from [JR] that you have justification for thinking 'S^1 is reliable'. Your justification for that claim can only come from an evidential source, and if it comes from a source whose own reliability is ultimately supported by a third source, then your justification for 'S^1 is reliable' will ultimately come from that third source. This is because the support relation between evidential sources is transitive.

The simplest justificatory structure would just involve S^1 justifying the claim 'S^1 is reliable'. In that case, S^N is just equivalent to S^1. Alternatively, the justificatory structure could involve several evidential sources, each supporting the reliability of the one before. Either way, the result is the same. Because your number of evidential sources is finite, it is inevitable that the justificatory structure supporting 'S^1 is reliable' will reach a stopping point. Hence:

7. ∴ There is a source S^N such that your justification for the claim 'S^1 is reliable' ultimately comes from S^N. [3, 4, 5, 6]

So S^N can be identified as is just whatever source ultimately provides you with justification for the claim 'S^1 is reliable'. And because it does, [JR] entails that you have justification for thinking 'S^N is reliable':

8. ∴ You have justification for the claim 'S^N is reliable'. [1, 7]

Again, your justification for 'S^N is reliable' must come from an evidential source. But we have already identified S^N as the source which ultimately supports S^1. So there can be no further source to ultimately support S^N, otherwise S^N wouldn't *ultimately* support S^1. So your justification for the claim 'S^N is reliable' ultimately comes from S^N.

This means that either your justification for 'S^N is reliable' directly comes from S^N, or directly from a source whose own reliability is ultimately supported by S^N. But the result is the same in either case. It follows that S^N ultimately provides justification for a claim affirming its own reliability:

9. ∴ Either S^N provides you with justification for the claim 'S^N is reliable' directly, or a source whose reliability is supported by S^N provides you with justification for the claim 'S^N is reliable'. [4, 5, 6, 8]

10. ∴ If a source whose reliability is supported by S^N provides you with justification for the claim 'S^N is reliable', then S^N ultimately provides you with justification for the claim 'S^N is reliable'. [5]

11. ∴ S^N provides you with justification for the claim 'S^N is reliable'. [8, 9, 10]

In addition, it's safe to say that justification for an evidential source's reliability counts as justification for its justificatory efficacy. After all, your evidence for a claim is just whatever makes it likely that the claim is true. So the kind of justification you gain from evidential sources aims at truth. And reason to think that a source is reliable is reason to think that beliefs based on that source are likely to be true. For this reason, justification for a source's reliability counts as justification for its justificatory efficacy.

Some theories go so far as to equate justification with reliability. Earlier we considered process reliabilism, which says that justification just is causation by a reliable process. But we don't have to go so far as to equate the two properties. All we need to say is that having justification to think an evidential source reliable is sufficient for having justification to think that it is a source of justification:

12. If S^N provides you with justification for the claim 'S^N is reliable', then S^N provides you with justification for the claim 'S^N is a justification source'. [Premise]

13. ∴ S^N provides you with justification for the claim 'S^N is a justification source'. [11, 12]

It follows that S^N provides an instance of epistemically circular justification. After all, I defined the notion of epistemically circular justification I'm working with as follows:

14. [EC-J]: An instance of epistemically circular justification is one in which a justification source S provides you with justification for the claim 'S is a justification source'. [Premise]

So it is a simple matter to infer:

15. ∴ If S^N provides you with justification for the claim 'S^N is a justification source', then epistemically circular justification is possible. [14]

16. ∴ Epistemically circular justification is possible. [13, 15]

It is clear that affirming [JR], together with several very plausible principles, commits you to thinking that epistemically circular justification is possible. So the Problem of the Criterion is a problem for defenders of [JR] who wish to avoid this commitment. But the Argument from Evidential Circularity doesn't trade on affirming [JR]. So far we have only treated [JR] as an assumption in the course of showing that it commits its defenders to epistemic circularity. This means we can now discharge the assumption and say that:

17. ∴ If [JR] is correct, then epistemically circular justification is possible.

[Suppositional reasoning from 1-16; Assumption 1 Discharged]

This gives us the first horn of the dilemma. Our next task is to see why a commitment to the possibility of epistemically circular justification follows from the negation of [JR] as well.

1.3 The Bootstrapping Problem

The Problem of the Criterion might seem like a reason to reject [JR]. That principle imposes a special requirement on gaining justification from an evidential source, but it should be unsurprising that the requirement it imposes generates further requirements of its own. Because it seems you can only gain justification for an evidential source's reliability from another source, whose reliability you then need to also verify, making justification for reliability a prerequisite for gaining justification from the original source starts us off on a regress from which epistemic circularity is the only escape. And it is usually thought that circular justification is impossible.

For this reason, many theories of justification reject [JR]. According to those theories:

> [~JR]: There is an evidential source G such that G provides you with justification even when you lack justification for the claim 'G is reliable'.

Following terminology introduced by Cohen (2002), we can call sources which fit this description 'basic justification sources'. Accordingly, let us call theories that accept [~JR] 'basic justification theories.'

Many widely-discussed theories of justification count as basic justification theories. Earlier, we considered process reliabilism, which equates the justification of a belief with being caused or sustained by a reliable process (see Goldman 1979, 2008). According to process reliabilists, you don't need to also have justification for *thinking* that the process is reliable. As long as your beliefs *really are* reliably caused, they will be justified.

Process reliabilism is a classic example of an externalist theory, one which denies that the conditions responsible for justification are always internally accessible mental states. But there are internalist theories which allow basic justification as well. One version is James Pryor's (2000) dogmatism. According to Pryor, whenever you have an experience as of something's being the case, you thereby have immediate *prima facie* justification to believe that it is the case. For instance, your visual experience that there is text in front of you gives you *prima facie* justification to believe that there is. And this is so whether or not you have justification for thinking your visual experiences reliable.

A very similar theory is Michael Huemer's (2001, 2007) phenomenal conservatism. According to Huemer, if it seems to you that something is the case, then (in the absence of defeaters) you have some degree of justification to believe that it is the case. So you have some degree of justification to believe that there is text in front of you as long as it seems to you that there is. Again, this doesn't require that you have justification for thinking your visual seemings reliably indicate the world.

Of course, these views don't exhaust the range of defensible basic justification theories. But they do represent contemporary examples of theories which trade on denying [JR].

So why does denying [JR] commit you to the possibility of epistemically circular justification? The reason is as follows. [~JR] is the claim that there is an evidential source which can provide you with justification even when you lack justification for its reliability. But any source of which this is true can quickly generate evidence for its reliability anyway, through a procedure called 'bootstrapping'.

To see how this works, let's examine what a bootstrapping inference looks like. Bootstrapping was named and popularised as a subject of debate by Vogel (2000), though earlier versions were discussed by Alston (1986) and Fumerton (1995). We'll stick with the example that Vogel uses, with only slight modifications.

Vogel describes a driver named Roxanne, whose car features a highly reliable gas gauge. Although Roxanne treats this gauge as an indication of the state of her fuel tank, she actually has no evidence at all about its reliability. By Vogel's stipulation, she simply goes by what it says, without giving even a thought to whether it is reliable.

This means that she forms justified beliefs in the following manner. On an occasion when the gauge indicates that the tank is full, Roxanne forms the belief:

i. According to my gauge, my tank is full at present. [Premise]

But Roxanne doesn't just form a belief about what the gauge says. She also happens to form a belief about the state of the tank, namely:

ii. My tank is full at present. [Premise]

We don't need to assume that Roxanne actually *infers* [ii] from [i]. She just looks at the gauge, forms a belief about the tank, and also happens to form a separate belief about the gauge. And even though she happens to implicitly trust the gauge in practice, at no point does she actually consider the question of its general reliability.

If [~JR] is true, then [i] and [ii] can count as justified, though the details of what makes them justified will vary depending on which basic justification theory we choose to work with. Vogel's original example dealt with reliabilism, so we can treat that as our background theory for present purposes. On the reliabilist view, [i] and [ii] are justified by the fact that Roxanne's gauge and vision are both highly reliable. But it would be easy to describe the example in terms of other theories as well: for instance, [i] and [ii] could be justified according to Pryor's dogmatism or Huemer's phenomenal conservatism, simply in virtue of the fact that they seem true to Roxanne.

So now Roxanne has a justified belief that her tank is full, and a justified belief that her gauge says it is. From the claim 'my tank is full at present', Roxanne can infer that:

iii. ∴ 'My tank is full at present' is correct. [ii]

From here, it is a straightforward matter for Roxanne to confirm that what her gauge says is actually correct:

iv. ∴ What my gauge says is correct on this occasion. [i, iii]

This result should be surprising! Simply by taking a look at the gauge, Roxanne has obtained grounds to confirm justifiably that what the gauge says is actually right.

But the problem is not just Roxanne's ability to confirm justifiably that her gauge is right in a single instance. As long as the gauge continues to provide justification, Roxanne can carry out exactly the same procedure many times over. For example, when the gauge indicates that the tank is empty, Roxanne will be able to form a justified belief that it is and a justified belief that the gauge says it is. Again, she will be able to use these beliefs to arrive at the justified conclusion that it is correct.

Let us imagine that Roxanne does in fact conduct inferences of the same form as [i-iv] in a large number of cases. We can abbreviate their conclusions as a single premise:

v. [conclusions derived from many more inferences of the form i-iv] [Premise]

These conclusions count as a large amount of evidence about the gauge's reliability. Because bootstrapping is a kind of self-corroboration, the evidence will always indicate that the gauge is correct. So by induction from this evidential base, Roxanne can infer:

vi. ∴ What my gauge says is always correct. [Induction from iv, v]

vii. ∴ My gauge is reliable. [vi]

To say that an evidential source is reliable is to say that it tends to accurately reflect the world, at least in most ordinary circumstances. I have already pointed out that this is a modal claim and not just a claim about its previous track record. But an extensive perfect track record does count as good inductive evidence that the source will continue to be correct in future. So it counts as good inductive evidence for the source's reliability.

It is easy to be distracted by background features of Vogel's example. Hardly anyone has no evidence at all about the reliability of an average car's gas gauge. And it is easy to point out that Roxanne should use a better means for verifying the gauge's reliability: for instance, she could use a dipstick to check the tank's fuel level and compare it with the gauge. But what the case illustrates is a general structural observation about basic justification. As long as there is an evidential source which can provide basic justification, and as long as it is possible to have true justified beliefs about what it says, then it is possible to bootstrap to the justified conclusion that the source is reliable.

Vogel (2000) and Fumerton (1995) originally proposed the Bootstrapping Problem as a reason to reject reliabilism, on the grounds that no reasonable theory could allow you to confirm a source's reliability just by trusting it. So it was some embarrassment when Cohen (2002) pointed out that the problem generalises to all theories which deny [JR] (including Vogel's and Fumerton's!) Any defensible basic justification theory allows the possibility of bootstrapping, because basic justification sources allow you to very easily gain the kind of evidence which confirms their reliability.[11]

Bootstrapping is only a problem for theories which deny [JR]. If [JR] is true, then bootstrapping is impossible for the following reason: in order to gain justification from an evidential source, you need to *already* have justification for thinking it reliable. So you won't be able to gain any new epistemically circular justification by bootstrapping. [JR] would make it the case that you can only justify the premises of a bootstrapping argument if you are antecedently justified in believing the conclusion (Cohen 2002).

Of course, reliability comes in degrees. Can you use a bootstrapping inference to *increase* the degree of reliability you can justifiably ascribe to your source, even if you already have justification to think it reliable?

If [JR] is true, this isn't possible either. If *whether* you have justification for a source's reliability is relevant to its justificatory efficacy, then *how much* reliability you can ascribe to it should be relevant as well. That is, the degree of reliability you can antecedently ascribe to your source will limit the strength of the evidence you can gain by trusting it. The result is that as long as [JR] is true, a bootstrapping inference cannot increase your justification for the source's reliability (Barnett, 2014).

[11] Cohen's original observation was about basic knowledge rather than basic justification: see my qualification at the end of Section 1.1.

To see this, imagine that [JR] is true and that Roxanne is antecedently justified in thinking her gauge is, say, 90% reliable. When she bootstraps, she ends up with a large sample of cases in which she found that it was correct. But if she is only justified in believing that the gauge is 90% reliable, then she is really only justified in believing each individual claim about the gauge's correctness with 90% credence – that is, she is justified in believing that each claim is only 90% likely to be correct. And when these claims are used as evidence from which she performs her induction, she is only justified in believing that the gauge was correct 90% of the time. Her prior justification for its reliability limits her overall ability to perform induction on the evidence. So bootstrapping is possible if and only if [~JR] is true.[12]

Having seen what bootstrapping involves, let us formulate the remaining branch of the Argument from Evidential Circularity as follows. We can begin by assuming:

18. [~JR]: There is an evidential source G such that G provides you with justification even when you lack justification for the claim 'G is reliable'.

[Assumed]

Although Vogel's example is formulated in terms of a very specific source (Roxanne's gauge), it is likely that the evidential sources which fit G's description include fundamental sources like vision, hearing, touch or memory. Ultimately, our other evidence about the world is acquired through these faculties. Their reliability is not guaranteed, but if any sources can give us justification in the absence of our having justification for thinking that they are reliable, it should be these ones.

[12] Weisberg (2010) argues that bootstrapping does allow you to gain knowledge that your source was more reliable than you initially thought. But Barnett (2014) has developed a formal model of the constraint I describe above, which he uses to convincingly refute Weisberg's view. Note also that the Argument from Evidential Circularity isn't vitiated even if Weisberg is right.

Of course, there wouldn't be much use in affirming [~JR] unless we also thought that our basic justification sources actually provide justification in many cases! Otherwise, recourse to [~JR] as a component in an overall theory of justification would do little towards explaining how we can actually gain a coherent and justified view of the world, which is part of the motivation for developing such a theory in the first place.

So the proponent of [~JR] should allow that G can justify a set of propositions P^1 – P^N, where N is at least the minimum number of justified beliefs about G's correctness in particular cases that you need in order to inductively establish that G is generally reliable. Since each of these claims is logically equivalent to a claim affirming that it is correct, G can provide you with justification for those claims as well:

19. If [~JR] then G can provide you with justification for claims P^1 - P^N. [Premise]
20. ∴ G can provide you with justification for claims P^1 - P^N. [18, 19]
21. Each of P^1 - P^N entails a claim affirming that it is correct. [Premise]
22. ∴ G can provide you with justification for claims affirming that P^1 - P^N are all correct. [20, 21]

In addition, the proponent of [~JR] should allow that you can have justified beliefs affirming that P^1 – P^N are each outputs of G. As we've seen, the sources most likely to fit G's description are fundamental ones like perception, hearing, touch, and memory. It is possible for us to have justified beliefs about what they seem to indicate, even when we don't have justification for thinking those indications reliable. So:

23. You have justification for claims affirming that P^1 - P^N are each outputs of G. [Premise]

From here, it is a straightforward matter to infer that G provides you with justification to believe that it is correct about each of $P^1 - P^N$. And from that evidential base, you will be able to inductively establish that G is reliable, in just the same way Roxanne did:

24. ∴ G can provide you with justification for claims affirming that G is correct about each of P^1 - P^N. [22, 23]

25. Claims affirming that G is correct about each of P^1 - P^N jointly inductively entail that 'G is reliable'. [Premise]

26. ∴ G can provide you with justification for the claim 'G is reliable'. [24, 25]

As I have pointed out, your evidence for a claim is just whatever makes it more likely that the claim is true. And reason to think that a source is reliable is reason to think that beliefs based on that source are likely to be true. For this reason, having justification for a source's reliability is sufficient for having justification for its justificatory efficacy:

27. If G provides you with justification for the claim 'G is reliable', then G provides you with justification for the claim 'G is a justification source'. [Premise]

28. ∴ G can provide you with justification for the claim 'G is a justification source'. [26, 27]

Since I have defined an epistemically circular instance of justification as one in which a source of justification justifies the claim that it provides justification, it follows that the proponent of [~JR] is committed to the possibility of epistemic circularity:

29. [EC-J]: An instance of epistemically circular justification is one in which a justification source S provides you with justification for the claim 'S is a justification source'. [Premise]

30. ∴ If G can provide you with justification for the claim 'G is a justification source', then epistemically circular justification is possible. [29]

31. ∴ Epistemically circular justification is possible. [28, 30]

This consequence – which has become known as the 'Bootstrapping Problem' – is an embarrassment for the proponent of [~JR] who wishes to maintain that circular justification is impossible. But the Argument from Evidential Circularity doesn't trade on affirming [~JR]. Having assumed [~JR] for the sake of argument, we can now discharge that assumption and assert simply that:

32. ∴ If [~JR] is correct, then epistemically circular justification is possible.
[Suppositional reasoning from 18-31; Assumption 18 Discharged]

As we saw in Section 1.2, commitment to the possibility of circular justification follows from [JR] also. So as long as the premises of the argument are correct, we can simply suspend judgement about whether [JR] is true, and conclude that:

33. ∴ Epistemically circular justification is possible. [17, 32]

1.4 Responding to Evidential Circularity

The Argument from Evidential Circularity represents a challenge for any theory which allows you to gain justification from an evidential source. The problem concerns [JR]: the view that an evidential source can only provide justification if you are justified in thinking it reliable. We saw in Section 1.2 that affirming [JR] starts you off on an infinite regress from which epistemic circularity is the only escape. And we saw in Section 1.3 that denying [JR] allows you to confirm your source's reliability by bootstrapping. Since having justification for an evidential source's reliability is sufficient for having justification for its justificatory efficacy, the result is that epistemically circular justification is possible whether or not [JR] is true.

Let us consider how we ought to respond to the Argument from Evidential Circularity. The simplest response would be simply to accept that epistemically circular justification is possible.[13] However, I pointed out in my Introduction that accepting circularity exposes us to two challenges.

In the first place, circular arguments are dialectically ineffective: if I try to show you that a source provides justification by relying on evidence drawn from that source, it seems that you should not be persuaded by my argument. If you don't already agree with me, then you have no reason to accept my premises; and if you do already agree with me, then you simply don't need persuading. So it looks like nothing ought to be accomplished by an epistemically circular argument.

[13] Alston (1986, 1993, 2005), Bergmann (2000, 2004), Schmitt (2004) and Van Cleve (1979, 2003), accept this conclusion.

The dialectical ineffectiveness problem is most acute in the context of debate with the sceptic. It seems much too easy to just rely on our evidential sources to show that they give us justified beliefs. Surely, proving that we do is harder than that!

Richard Fumerton articulates this point forcefully:

> You cannot *use* perception to justify the reliability of perception! You cannot *use* memory to justify the reliability of memory! You cannot *use* induction to justify the reliability of induction! Such attempts to respond to the skeptic's concerns involve blatant, indeed pathetic, circularity. [Fumerton 1995, pg. 177]

The second reason for being suspicious of circular justification is the prospect of 'bad company'. If it's always possible to justify a source's efficacy by trusting it, then it looks like all kinds of dodgy sources can be justified. We would, for instance, be able to use gambler's fallacious reasoning to show that such reasoning will work in future because it hasn't worked in the past. And we would be able to show that the mystical guru is trustworthy just by trusting his pronouncements. The fact that these justifications would be circular seems relevant to an explanation of why they fail.

But the two problems are not independent. Together, they generate the possibility that proponents of radically different evidential sources – for instance, the scientific method and revealed scripture – could end up in entirely closed-off epistemic systems. If it's possible to justify two sets of different evidential sources in a circular fashion, and impossible to get any dialectical traction on proponents of different sources, then we might worry that epistemic circularity is an impediment to our ability to resolve disagreements over justification by rational debate. Since philosophy has traditionally proceeded by that method, this looks like a serious methodological problem.

Of course, no one wants to allow that all instances of apparent epistemically circular justification are genuine. And that isn't what the Argument from Evidential Circularity tries to show. But if some sources can legitimately justify themselves and some cannot, then we will need to explain what distinguishes permissible from impermissible cases. And that looks like a hard question.

I will return to this question in Section 5.3, but first I think it is worth considering how we might refute the Argument from Evidential Circularity. Since it is more common to deny [JR] than to accept it, most existing responses focus on the Bootstrapping Problem. A variety of proposals have been developed in the past couple of years for how we might be able to endorse a basic justification theory whilst avoiding the consequence that basic justification sources can verify their own efficacy. There might be a proposal of this kind which is successful, but this isn't the type of response I want to focus on. Instead, I want to investigate a line of response which I think has been under-examined, and which addresses the Problem of the Criterion.

In the next three Chapters I will look at the prospects for tackling the Problem of the Criterion by appealing to pragmatism about justification. This is the view that prudential considerations can sometimes make you justified in believing certain claims even when you lack sufficient evidence for them. This will allow us to avoid the Problem of the Criterion by rejecting the idea that the reliability of an evidential source can only be justified by evidence. In Chapter Two I'll look at an existing version of this approach developed by Byeong Lee (2014), then in Chapter Three I will make substantial modifications to Lee's proposal. In Chapter Four I will raise a novel problem closely related to bootstrapping, and develop a solution. Later, in Chapter Five, I'll present my own argument for thinking that circular justification is possible.

Chapter Two: A Pragmatic Response

In Section 1.2, it was argued that endorsing [JR] presents us with a version of the ancient Problem of the Criterion. This is because it looks like claims affirming the reliability of our sources can only be justified by evidence. But if [JR] applies to every evidential source, then we are off on an infinite regress from which circularity is the only escape. Since the number of our sources is finite, some source will ultimately provide justification for the claim that it is a source of justification. And it is usually thought that circular justification is impossible.

Byeong Lee (2014) thinks that this problem makes it impossible to establish that our evidential sources are reliable by conventional means (pg. 415). Nonetheless, he maintains that this result is not an epistemic disaster. Even if we cannot directly show that our sources are reliable without falling into circularity, we nevertheless have good reason to treat them as such. By appealing to the relationship between our evidential sources and our epistemic goals, Lee argues that we can gain justification from our sources without having to allow epistemic circularity.

Lee's argument depends upon taking a goal-oriented pragmatic view of justification. In Section 2.1 I will explain this view in more detail and offer some motivations for accepting it. In Section 2.2 I will go over Lee's argument and consider its implications as a response to the Problem of the Criterion (and hence, to the Argument from Evidential Circularity). In Section 2.3 I'll argue that Lee's particular version of this approach fails, although I think his general strategy is on the right track. So I will make some modifications to Lee's proposal in Chapter Three.

2.1 Pragmatism about Justification

Pragmatism about justification is the view that prudential considerations can make you justified in believing claims, even when you don't have sufficient evidence for them. If holding a particular belief will help you accomplish a particular goal, then the pragmatist view is that the belief is justified for you insofar as it helps you achieve that goal. Since believing seems like a kind of cognitive action, the proposal is that the standards of prudential justification used to evaluate ordinary actions can extend to the evaluation of beliefs.[14]

Let's consider an example. Suppose that you are running in a race, which you desperately want to win. You don't have any evidence about how likely you are to win – for instance, evidence about how your athletic ability compares with that of your competitors. Nonetheless, you know that if you form the belief 'I am going to win this race', you'll feel more confident and perform better. Consequently, having the belief 'I am going to win this race' will make it more likely that you will win. All else being equal, it seems like you have some justification to believe it.

That's meant to be a case where you have justification to believe something even when you don't have sufficient evidence for it. But it is easy to point out that in forming the belief that you will win, you are actually gaining a kind of evidence. Since having the belief raises your actual chances of winning, and you know this, it ought to increase your non-prudential grounds for thinking that you'll win as well. In effect, the occurrence of the belief counts as evidence for its own content.

[14] For classic defences of pragmatism, see Pascal (1670: 1978) and James (1896: 1962). For recent ones, see Reisner (2008, 2009) and Marušić (2011, 2012, 2013). Pragmatism might also be interpreted as an account of rational belief rather than justification. The arguments I discuss should work on either reading.

To see this, consider things from the perspective of an outside observer. The outsider has no information about the athletes' relative abilities, or other pertinent information, except the knowledge that *this* participant has the advantage of an optimistic outlook. The only difference between you and the observer is that you know that *you* are the athlete in question. So once you form the belief, you have both prudential and evidential reasons for maintaining it.[15]

However, the important point is that it is your prudential interest in winning, not your evidence, which ultimately makes your belief justified. For one thing, the evidence that you gain by forming the belief could still be insufficient to justify it on evidential grounds alone. That is, an outside observer who shared your evidence but not your prudential interests might lack *sufficient* justification to believe that you'll win. And for another thing, it seems like some beliefs can be justified *in spite of* the evidence - that is, in cases where you have good evidence that your belief is actually false.

Consider another example, adapted slightly from Andrew Reisner (2008, pg. 25). Suppose that you are in hospital suffering from a terrible illness. You know that in your present state you only have a 10% chance of survival, but that you can double this chance if you form the belief 'I will survive this illness'. Surely, it would seem, you ought to form that belief! And it seems like you should form it even though your total evidence counts against it. Not only do you have a 90% chance of dying now, before believing it, but you will have an 80% chance of dying from the illness even when you do believe it. So it looks like this is a case in which your prudential interest in surviving makes you justified in believing that you will, even when you have good evidence that the belief is actually false.

---

[15] See James (1896: 1962, pp. 54-56) and Foley (1991, pg. 101) for related discussions.

This example provides better intuitive support for pragmatism than the first one, because it shows that what justifies your beliefs can sometimes be unrelated to your evidence, even if you do sometimes gain evidence as a side-effect. It seems that in the hospital case, your prudential reasons for belief *override* your evidential ones. They not only provide prudential justification to believe 'I will survive this illness', they make believing it all-things-considered *rational* as well. It is not as if your belief is prudentially justified, evidentially unjustified, and there is no further question of which is more important.[16] In the hospital case especially, it seems like prudential justification is the overriding consideration.

These two examples might seem a little far-fetched. But Berislav Marušić (2011, 2012, 2013) has argued that pragmatism also provides the best explanation of what we should believe whenever we commit to undertaking difficult actions. Whenever we promise or intend to do something that we know is hard, our promises and our intentions should be sincere. But neither a promise nor an intention can be sincere, according to Marušić, unless we actually believe that we will do what we promise or intend to. If we know that the action is difficult, we have evidence that we won't succeed in doing it. So it seems that we ought to believe against the evidence whenever we rationally promise or intend to do something difficult.

Marušić gives the following example (2012, pg. 2). Suppose you decide to quit smoking. Your decision to do so is rational, let's suppose, and your intention is sincere: you have thrown away your cigarettes, told everyone that you are quitting, and read a self-help book on how to beat the habit. So it would be rather odd if you were to say something like 'I am not going to smoke anymore, but I might smoke.' It would seem to betray a lack of sincerity. Nonetheless, the data on quitting isn't very encouraging.

[16] Feldman (2000 pp. 691-695) seems to take this position.

According to the American Medical Association: "Most ex-smokers try several times, often as many as 8 to 10 times, before they are able to quit for good" (Brender 2006, cited by Marušić 2012). So it looks like this is a case in which you have evidence that you won't succeed but overriding prudential reasons to believe that you will. If Marušić is right that sincere intention requires belief, then it looks like you what you ought to do when you try to quit smoking is to believe against the evidence.

So the pragmatic account provides an explanation for justified belief which goes beyond evidential considerations. Of course, the pragmatist isn't committed to saying that our beliefs *never* ought to respect the evidence. Even if the norms of justification are ultimately prudential, what we are prudentially justified in believing is probably just what the evidence supports, most of the time. We need to make decisions about how to interact with the world, and this requires having accurate information. But the pragmatist claim is that there are circumstances in which the evidence does not have the final say. If we are to remain optimistic in the face of hardship, or think ourselves capable of performing difficult actions, then it looks like we occasionally need to believe against the evidence.

A common objection to pragmatism (which we can call the 'involuntarist objection') runs as follows. Pragmatism makes a claim about what you ought to believe. But thinking that you 'ought' to believe something commits you to thinking that you can make a voluntary choice about whether to believe it. And it doesn't look like we can ever believe or disbelieve something just by choosing to. So we should reject the pragmatic view of justification.[17]

[17] See Feldman (2000), Hookway (2000, pg. 60), Kelly (2002, pg. 6) and Williams (1973) for discussion.

I think the involuntarist objection fails for three reasons. In the first place, pragmatism concerns the content of your beliefs, not their etiology. Although pragmatism does make claims about what you ought to believe, these should not be taken as the kind of 'ought' claims that entail your ability to believe things by voluntarily choosing to. It is enough for the pragmatist just to hold that believing some propositions is better than believing others, regardless of how to you come to believe them. For instance, you might involuntarily come to believe something just by realising that it is the prudentially rational thing to believe, without any conscious act of will on your part, in much the same way as in ordinary cases you might involuntarily form a belief in response to decisive evidence. Pragmatism is to be understood as a claim about what it is better and worse to *end up* believing, whatever the etiological details of your beliefs.[18]

Secondly, the involuntarist objection doesn't provide a reason to reject pragmatism *per se*, even if the claim that you ought to believe something did entail that you can believe it voluntarily. If this were the case, then the involuntarist objection would provide a reason to reject *any* theory of what you ought to believe. That is, no normative theory of rational belief or justification could be plausible if doxastic normativity requires belief to be under our voluntary control. But even non-pragmatists usually think that there are some things it is better to believe and some things it is worse to believe, even if they reject the pragmatic explanation of why. So as long as we are interested in getting *any* normative account of rational belief or justification, we have reason to reject the involuntarist objection.[19]

---

[18] Marušić (2011, pp. 35-36; 2012, pp. 24-25) makes a similar point.

[19] Reisner (2009) makes a related point, with a special focus on pragmatism's traditional rival evidentialism.

Thirdly, there is reason to think that the involuntarist objection is self-defeating. Either the involuntarist thinks we ought to believe that pragmatism fails to provide a plausible account of justification, or they don't. If they don't, it is hard to see what the upshot of their objection really is. But if they do think that we ought to believe pragmatism fails, then either this 'ought' requires voluntary control over our beliefs or it doesn't. If it does, the involuntarist is in trouble! For their claim is that voluntary control over belief is impossible. And if it doesn't, then the involuntarist must concede that there are some normative claims about belief that don't require us to have voluntary control – in which case, they must allow that the pragmatist's normative claims can be of this kind also.[20]

2.2 Byeong Lee's Argument

Pragmatism about justification provides us with a means of avoiding the Problem of the Criterion, and hence with a response to the Argument from Evidential Circularity. As we saw in Section 1.2, the Problem of the Criterion arises from affirming the requirement that you need to have justification for thinking an evidential source reliable if it is to provide justification, as well as the requirement that you can only gain justification for a source's reliability from evidence. If we endorse pragmatism about justification, we can avoid this problem by denying that justification for thinking a source reliable can only come from evidence. In this Section, I will consider a version of this response which has been developed by Byeong Lee (2014).[21]

[20] In Section 4.2, I will distinguish normative claims about what to believe from normative claims about what to consciously direct your attention to. This further strengthens my response to involuntarism.
[21] Lee doesn't use the phrase 'pragmatism' to describe his view explicitly, but his argument only works if we agree that our goals and interests can justify our beliefs – so we can charitably ascribe the pragmatist view to him.

Lee argues that we have a reason to accept the general reliability of our perceptual, memorial and introspective judgements because doing so is the best way for us to achieve our epistemic goal. He identifies this goal as:

> [T]o acquire correct information about the world in such a way that reduces the risk of getting incorrect information. [Lee 2014, pg. 417]

Lee's idea is that we should treat our sources as reliable because they provide us with the best chance of achieving this goal. Of course, the argument will only justify our evidential sources if pursuing our epistemic goal is actually reasonable. So Lee offers three reasons for thinking that it is.

The first reason is that correct information about the world is necessary for us to maintain our survival and welfare. Since having correct information is necessary for knowing what to avoid and what to obtain in the world, the epistemic goal can be considered prudentially reasonable.

A second reason is that correct information about the world is necessary for us to pursue our moral obligations. Lee cites Wilfrid Sellars' claim that:

> [I]t is because truth is a necessary condition of securing the common good that the search for it presents itself to us, on reflection, as categorically reasonable—in the truest sense a moral obligation. [Sellars 1974b, pp. 437-438]

The idea here is that we have obligations as members of a moral community, and that it is categorically reasonable to try to meet these obligations. Since trying to meet them requires having sufficiently good information about the world to enable moral decision-making, the epistemic goal can be regarded as categorically reasonable as well.

However, Lee's main argument for the reasonableness of our epistemic goal concerns its status as a presupposition of rational inquiry. The idea is that it is impossible to inquire rationally after the truth of any claim unless it is assumed at minimum that it is reasonable to care about whether it is true. To engage in inquiry without making this assumption would seem to involve a kind of practical self-contradiction, for it would seem that the reasonableness of the goal could not rationally be denied without the implicit assumption that the denier cares about the truth of whether the goal is reasonable. So it would seem that denying the reasonableness of our epistemic goal would be irrational (pp. 419-421).

Hence, Lee thinks, the epistemic goal must be regarded as reasonable, at least from the outset. Even a global sceptic will need to grant that it is worthwhile (at least for the sake of argument) to pursue the epistemic goal in order to engage in rational discourse with a non-sceptic:

> [If] the skeptic denies the epistemic presumption, she thereby denies the conceptual framework within which giving reasons, grounds, and justification takes place. Hence, even the skeptic must accept our epistemic presumption (at least for the sake of argument) to engage in epistemic discourse with us. [Lee 2014, pg. 421]

Of course, it is worth noting that the sceptic only has to assume the reasonableness of our epistemic goal at the outset: it might be possible for the sceptic to show that epistemic discourse turns out to be unreasonable even on its own terms. But the burden of proof for that claim, according to Lee, is on the sceptic. And it isn't a burden he thinks the sceptic can meet.

Having defended the reasonableness of pursuing our epistemic goal, Lee's next claim is that the best means of pursuing it involves trusting the deliverances of our evidential sources. Our perceptual faculties have the best chance, as far as we can tell, of providing reliable evidence about the external world. Similarly, our memorial and introspective faculties provide the best chance of providing reliable information about the past and about our internal mental states. As long as these are the best sources of evidence we've got with respect to the domains in question, it shouldn't matter that their reliability is not absolutely guaranteed.

Lee supports the claim that the evidential sources in question are the best we've got by pointing out that trusting them allows us to maximise the explanatory coherence of our conceptual framework. By relying on them, we can make successful predictions and reduce the number of unexplained observations. And they also allow us to construct explanations which cohere with the observations of other observers (pp. 422-423).

This puts Lee in a position to justify accepting the reliability of our evidential sources via the following simple argument. It represents a familiar pattern of practical reasoning from ends to means. Here is the example he provides for perception:

1. It is reasonable for us to pursue the epistemic goal. [Premise]
2. The best means of bringing about the epistemic goal requires accepting the general reliability of our perceptual judgments. [Premise]
3. ∴ It is reasonable for us to accept the general reliability of our perceptual judgments. [1,2]

[Lee 2014, pg. 422; adapted very slightly]

There are a few things to note about Lee's argument. Firstly, his isn't a theoretical argument which attempts to show that our perceptual judgements *are* reliable, but a practical argument which attempts to show that it is reasonable for us to *treat* them as such. The upshot of this argument though, according to Lee, is the same as if we had an argument which did establish that our perceptual judgements are reliable. Because it is reasonable for us to accept their reliability in pursuit of our epistemic goal, and because Lee takes the view that justification is essentially a goal-oriented concept, he thinks that our perceptual faculties can provide us with justification for their outputs.

The second thing to note is that although Lee does pitch his argument as a response to a version of the Problem of the Criterion, he neither gives a precise formulation of that problem (as I did in Section 1.2) nor considers the other branch of the Argument from Evidential Circularity (as I did in Section 1.3). So it will be worth saying a little more in order to accommodate his argument charitably in terms of the formulation I provided in Chapter One.

One way of interpreting Lee's conclusion is as a denial of [JR] – that is, as a denial of the claim that you require justification for thinking an evidential source reliable if you are to gain justification from it. On this reading, Lee would be proposing a theory on which something's visually seeming to you to be a certain way provides you with justification for thinking that it is that way, even if you don't have justification to think that your visual perception is reliable. So the idea would be that you can justifiably *treat* your source as reliable (by believing in accordance with its outputs), even if don't justifiably believe that it is.

However, I don't think this reading is the most charitable one. It would amount to a standard 'basic justification' theory resembling Pryor's (2000) dogmatism or Huemer's (2001, 2007) phenomenal conservatism. But we saw in Section 1.3 that basic justification theories face the Bootstrapping Problem, and hence are committed to allowing epistemic circularity. Because Lee's stated motivation is to avoid circularity, it would be unfortunate if his view turned out to avoid the Problem of the Criterion only to countenance bootstrapping.

I think a more charitable interpretation of Lee's position (in terms of how I have formulated the Argument from Evidential Circularity) is as follows. Since Lee's argument addresses the Problem of the Criterion, which arises for proponents of [JR], we should assume that his position involves affirming [JR]. In addition, the Problem of the Criterion depends upon affirming the claim that you can only justify the reliability of an evidential source by evidence. This was premise [4] in my formulation:

> [4]: For any evidential source S, justification for the claim 'S is reliable' can only come from an evidential source.

Since Lee's argument rests upon the pragmatist view that your goals and interests can make you justified in believing something, and since he tries to show that it is reasonable for us to accept the general reliability of our evidential judgements, I think the most charitable way of interpreting Lee's position is as an affirmation of [JR] but a denial of [4]. So the idea is that you need justification for thinking that 'S is reliable' in order for S to justify its outputs, but you can justify thinking 'S is reliable' by appealing to your epistemic goals. This gives us a tidy and charitable way of using Lee's argument as a response to the Argument from Evidential Circularity, even though Lee himself doesn't use the same formulation that I've used.

A third thing to notice is that even though the justification Lee provides for thinking our sources reliable is goal-oriented, it is still 'epistemic' justification in an important sense. This is because its normative force comes from our epistemic goal, which is to acquire correct information (in such a manner as to avoid incorrect information). Even those who are suspicious of the pragmatist view that goals like 'winning a race' or 'recovering from illness' can justify beliefs do tend to think that belief ordinarily aims at the truth. So the idea that epistemic justification can be understood as a goal-oriented concept shouldn't be too strange, because the goal in question is still a distinctively epistemic one.

Accordingly, Lee claims to have provided not only an explanation of why it is reasonable to accept the general reliability of our evidential judgements, but an insight into the nature of epistemic justification. Our evidential sources provide epistemic justification because accepting their reliability is necessary for pursuing our epistemic goal; and our goal is reasonable because it is justified by broader prudential and moral considerations, as well as by its status as a rational presupposition.

Fourthly, note that although Lee's main example is perception, he does claim that the same type of argument can also justify the other evidential sources he considers:

> [P]erceptual, introspective and memory judgments have similar epistemic status in our conceptual framework. Thus, we can defend accepting the general reliability of our introspective and memory judgments in a similar way as we can defend accepting the general reliability of our perceptual judgments. [pg. 430]

I think this commits Lee to two more instances of the same argument form that he used for perception. I'll discus one of them later, in Section 3.3.

2.3 Some Problems with Lee's Argument

In Section 2.1, I outlined pragmatism about justification, which is the view that your goals and preferences can make you justified in believing something even when you lack sufficient evidence for it. In Section 2.2, I outlined an argument provided by Byeong Lee (2014) for thinking our evidential sources reliable, which takes a pragmatic goal-oriented approach to justification. This looks like it provides a potential response to the Problem of the Criterion outlined in Section 1.2, and hence to the Argument from Evidential Circularity. We can affirm [JR] with respect to our evidential sources, but deny that we can only justify their reliability by evidence.

In this Section I will critically examine Lee's argument. Although I think his basic approach is correct, I will argue that some elements of his account are faulty. However, my examination of Lee's argument in this Section will help me to make some useful revisions to his approach. I develop these in Chapter Three.

The first premise of Lee's argument for accepting the reliability of perception (and of analogous arguments that he might provide in support of other sources) is a premise affirming the reasonableness of our epistemic goal. Recall that he identifies this goal as the following:

> [T]o acquire correct information about the world in such a way that reduces the risk of getting incorrect information. [pg. 417]

Although I agree that this goal is reasonable, I do have some doubts about the considerations he provides for thinking that it is reasonable. My worry is that these considerations turn out to be either too weak, or to involve epistemic circularity.

The first reason Lee provides is the claim that having correct information about the world is necessary for us to pursue our survival and welfare. That is, '[o]ur survival and welfare can be in jeopardy in case we do not know what to avoid and what to obtain in the world' (pg. 417). The second is that having correct information is necessary for us to pursue what is morally required of us. Lee agrees with Sellars that 'truth is a necessary condition for securing the common good' (pg. 417). Since we are members of a moral community, we have a responsibility to acquire sufficient correct information to enable moral decision-making.

Although these claims look reasonable, they don't seem like the kinds of claims that can be justified without appealing to the sources Lee is trying to justify. Even if it can be known *a priori* that correct information is needed in order to fulfil our moral obligations, for instance, it cannot be known *a priori* that we have any such obligations. To say that we are members of a moral community, with moral obligations towards other members of that community, is to make a contingent empirical claim about the way the external world is. It involves asserting the existence of other beings. I cannot see how such a claim can be justified without the use of our evidential sources.

Similarly, I doubt whether Lee can adequately justify the claim that we need correct information in order to promote our survival and wellbeing. I agree that we are mortal beings whose survival depends upon provision of oxygen, water, and food. But again, this is a contingent empirical claim that depends upon generalising from what we have learned and observed. Its justification depends upon induction from past cases ('humans typically die when deprived of air/water/food for long enough'), as well as upon our knowledge of physiology. Justifying the belief that our survival and welfare depends upon pursuing some things and avoiding others requires making use of information gained by the use of our evidential sources.

If we rely on our perceptual faculties to justify the reasonableness of our epistemic goal, the pursuit of which requires accepting the reliability of our perceptual judgements, then we ultimately have a situation where perception provides justification for treating it as reliable. Of course, treating perception as reliable could mean actually believing the general claim 'our perceptual judgements are reliable', or it could mean simply believing particular perceptual judgements, such as 'there is text in front of me now', without believing this general claim. But neither interpretation will help us avoid circularity.

As I noted in Section 2.2, accepting our particular perceptual judgements without accepting the general claim 'perception is reliable' will not help us avoid circularity. What we would be buying into, in effect, would just be a basic justification theory by which perception could provide justification without our needing justification to think it generally reliable. But all basic justification theories allow bootstrapping: that is, they make it too easy to gain the kind of evidence you can use to show that your evidential source is reliable anyway.

Alternatively, if we do just believe 'our perceptual judgements are reliable' as the direct upshot of Lee's argument, we end up in the same position. We would have a situation in which perception justifies its own reliability. Since having justification for a source's reliability is sufficient for having justification for its justificatory efficacy, either way we get a situation whereby perception justifies its own justificatory efficacy. According to the definition I provided in Section 1.1, an instance of epistemic circularity is just one in which a source justifies the claim that it is a source of justification. And this amounts to an instance of epistemic circularity.

Accordingly, I think we cannot justify Lee's first premise by appealing to facts about our moral obligations or facts about what's necessary for our survival if we are to avoid circularity. Those facts are contingent empirical facts, which can only be ascertained by the use of the evidential sources which Lee is trying to justify.

However, neither an appeal to our moral obligations nor to our interests in survival is the main argument Lee provides in support of his first premise. His main argument concerns the status of our goal as an assumption for rational inquiry. Lee's view is that we can assume our epistemic goal is reasonable by default, since this assumption is necessary if we are to inquire rationally after anything at all. That is, our whole practice of giving and providing reasons for belief only makes sense to the extent that we think seeking the truth (in such a manner as to avoid error) is worthwhile. Even a sceptic will have to endorse it, Lee thinks, if they are to engage us in debate.

I think Lee's view here is basically right: it does seem like there is a type of practical self-contradiction that would be involved if someone maintained that it is true that it doesn't matter whether any beliefs are true. But I disagree with Lee over the ultimate significance of this insight. Even if endorsing the reasonableness of our epistemic goal is necessary for rational inquiry, I don't think it is necessary to endorse it in any strong sense. I don't think its status as a rational presupposition is anything near strong enough for this goal to do the kind of work Lee needs it to do. Let me explain this further.

Firstly, let's review the content of this goal. As Lee puts it, our epistemic goal is:

> [T]o acquire correct information about the world in such a way that reduces the risk of getting incorrect information. [Lee 2014, pg. 417]

Notice that what we have here are actually two separate goals. To acquire correct information and to avoid acquiring incorrect information are not the same thing.[22] To see this, consider what I ought to do if all I care about is having true beliefs – suppose I couldn't care less about false ones, no matter how many I might pick up along the way. What I ought to do, in that case, is just form as many beliefs as possible! Sure, I'll get a lot of false beliefs, but if *all I care about* is getting as many true ones as I can, this shouldn't matter to me at all.

Conversely, consider what I ought to do if all I care about is not having false beliefs. Suppose I couldn't care less about how many true ones I miss out on, as long as I don't believe anything falsely. Surely, what I ought to do would be to suspend judgement (in the Pyrrhonist fashion) about as many things as I possibly can! Of course, I'd miss out on a lot of true beliefs, but *all I care about* is avoiding the false, this shouldn't matter to me at all.

These examples demonstrate that seeking the true and avoiding the false are not different formulations of the same goal, but distinct goals which to some extent stand in tension. It's also important to notice that they don't do equal work in Lee's argument. In order for it to be reasonable for us to accept the reliability of perception, it is not enough for it just to be reasonable to avoid forming false perceptual beliefs. If that were all we cared about, we ought not to trust perception at all. Rather, Lee's argument only works if we aim to form true perceptual beliefs. We can only justify accepting the reliability of our perceptual faculties, as a means for getting true information about the world, if we actually have the reasonable goal of getting true information about the world.

[22] See James (1896: 1962, pp. 48-50) for discussion.

Of course, we can still endorse the reasonability of avoiding error. But the main point I want to make is that it is the reasonability of truth-seeking which does the major work in Lee's argument. And the reasonability of truth-seeking, even if it is a rational presupposition in a sense, is not a rational presupposition in a sense that is strong enough to justify our evidential sources just by itself.

To see this, let's consider a sceptic who doesn't care about having true beliefs about the external world, as long as they avoid having false ones. The sceptic maintains that we don't have justified beliefs about the external world either. Of course, the sceptic is a party to rational inquiry and rational discourse, and so Lee's claim is that they must affirm the reasonableness of our epistemic goal, at least for the sake of argument. For instance, when the sceptic affirms that you are not justified in believing certain things about the external world, it would seem that they must agree that it is reasonable to pursue the *truth* about what you are justified in believing. So there is a sense in which they must endorse the epistemic goal. But they don't need to go any further than that. Even if they must agree that it is reasonable to pursue truth with respect to what we are justified in believing about the external world, they don't have to agree that it is reasonable to pursue truth with respect to the external world itself.

We can make this point clearer by distinguishing between beliefs *with* perceptual content and beliefs *about* perceptual content. An example of a belief with perceptual content would be the following:

[H]: 'I have hands.'

A belief about perceptual content, by contrast, looks like this:

[~JH]: 'I am not justified in believing 'I have hands.''

It is hard to make sense of a sceptic who believes that [~JH] is true, and argues for it, whilst denying that it even matters whether [~JH] is true. So the sceptic we are imagining ought to be interested in truths of a kind. But this does not necessitate that the sceptic ought (just in virtue of engaging in rational inquiry) to care about beliefs like [H] itself. It might be the case that when it comes to beliefs with perceptual content, the sceptic cares only about avoiding error; and when it comes to beliefs about perceptual content, sometimes about believing the truth.

Imagining a sceptic of this persuasion gives us a reason for thinking that there is no particularly strong sense in which we need to endorse the reasonability of truth-seeking if we are to engage in rational inquiry. It would seem that such engagement does require us to at least implicitly assume that there are some truths worth seeking. But we do not need to assume, just in virtue of being inquirers, that all truths are. And we certainly do not need to assume either, *just in virtue of being inquirers*, that truths with perceptual (or other empirical) content are worth seeking.

The status of our epistemic goal as a rational presupposition can only justify accepting the reliability of our perceptual faculties if the presupposition is that seeking true beliefs *with perceptual content* is reasonable. I have argued that this is not the case. Even if the reasonableness of our epistemic goal is a rational presupposition, it isn't a presupposition in anything near a strong enough sense to justify Lee's first premise. In addition, Lee's other reasons for accepting this premise depend on evidence gained from the sources Lee tries to justify. So I conclude that the reasons Lee has offered in support of this premise are either too weak, or fail to avoid epistemic circularity.

Chapter Three: The Pragmatic Response Revised

In Chapter One I outlined the main extant argument for thinking that epistemically circular justification is possible - the Argument from Evidential Circularity. In Chapter Two I considered the prospects for a response to this argument which trades on a pragmatic view of justification. In Section 2.2 I outlined an existing version of this approach developed by Byeong Lee (2014), and in Section 2.3 I identified some flaws in his proposal. However, I think the underlying approach is basically right. In view of the flaws I have identified, salvaging Lee's argument will have to involve finding an alternative justification for the reasonability of our epistemic goal. In this Chapter I will consider two approaches, one of which is externalist in character and one of which is internalist.

I outline the externalist approach in Section 3.1. I don't think this is the best way to improve Lee's proposal, and I will argue to that effect by considering what Lee says against a very similar externalist move. These considerations might not be absolutely decisive, so those inclined towards externalism might be happy to accept the externalist proposal as it stands.

My own view is that we ought to find internally accessible reasons for thinking our evidential sources reliable. I will provide reasons of this kind in Section 3.2, which involve identifying our goal as a rational preference, as well as taking a broadly Humean view about the rational status of our preferences. Of course, our preferences are contingent psychological states, and the faculty by which we access those states is introspection. So in Section 3.3 I will defend the traditional view that we have a default entitlement to thinking our introspective faculties reliable.

3.1 An Externalist Approach

Lee's original reasons for thinking that the epistemic goal is reasonable included the claim that having accurate information is necessary if we are to pursue our survival, and the claim that accurate information is necessary if we are to adequately fulfil our moral obligations to others. I argued in Section 2.3 that the existence of our moral obligations and our physiological requirements for survival are contingent empirical claims which cannot be justified except by appealing to our evidential sources. So they cannot be used to justify a premise in Lee's argument for accepting the reliability of our sources without an instance of epistemic circularity. But whether we have justification to think our goal reasonable is one thing: whether it is in fact reasonable is another.

In order for claims about our survival interests or moral obligations to justify the reasonableness of our goal, and hence the reliability of our sources, we might be able to dispense with the idea that those claims themselves need to be justified. Presumably, what makes it the case that we ought to pursue truth is the *fact* that doing so is reasonable, not the justified belief that it is. Thus, we may be able to take the view that our goal is justified as long as truth-seeking *really is* prudentially or morally necessary. Whether we can prove that it is wouldn't seem to matter.

This type of appeal to external facts rather than to internal justified beliefs is characteristically a feature of externalist epistemologies.[23] Accordingly, let us call the response I have suggested the 'Externalist Appeal to our Goal'.

---

[23] This response borrows a move used by Van Cleve (1979) to justify an externalist form of foundationalism. See Shatz (1983) for a related discussion. Thanks also to Salman Panahi for suggesting that I consider the appeal to facts rather than justified beliefs to support the reasonableness of our goal.

I doubt that Lee himself would be particularly happy with this proposal. As I pointed out in Section 2.2, the most charitable way to interpret his position is to take him as endorsing [JR], and [JR] is usually more attractive to internalists than to externalists. In addition, Lee explicitly considers a similar externalist proposal and offers reasons for rejecting it. Accordingly, let us examine that proposal before considering whether his reasons against it also count against the Externalist Appeal to our Goal. Lee talks about externalism only briefly (pg. 414, footnote 1), so I'll charitably expand on his objections by providing a little more argumentative detail.

It is standard for externalists to deny that having justification for a source's reliability is necessary for it to provide justification. All that's needed, according to standard externalist views, is that the source is *in fact* reliable, or *in fact* tracks truth, or *in fact* meets a similar external condition. For the purposes of exposition, we can just treat 'reliability' as our example of a standard externalist condition for justification. Hence, the suggestion is that as long as your source really is reliable, beliefs formed in accordance with it are justified, whether or not you also have justification for thinking that it is reliable. Accordingly, let us call this proposal the 'Externalist Appeal to Reliability'.

The first problem Lee identifies with this approach is that it gives rise to a conditionality problem. If the fact that a source is reliable is what grants it justificatory efficacy, then it seems we can ascribe only a conditional justificatory status to beliefs supported by that source. That is, the best we can say of our visual beliefs, for instance, is that they are justified *if* our visual faculties are reliable. But since we can never step outside our own minds to check whether vision is actually reliable, the worry is that we cannot say for sure whether our visual beliefs are justified. We can only say 'they are justified *if* the right external conditions obtain'. But surely, we want be able to say more than this! It seems we want to know whether our beliefs really are justified. If all we can ascribe to them is conditional justification, then we haven't really obtained an answer to this question at all.[24]

The conditionality problem also gives rise to a bad company problem, which is Lee's main reason for rejecting the Externalist Appeal to Reliability. This is because conditional justification can be easily ascribed to all kinds of dodgy beliefs and evidential sources. Consider a source like a crystal ball gazing (the example is from Alston 1993, pg. 17). We can say exactly the same about beliefs formed by crystal ball gazing as we can about beliefs formed by regular visual perception: that they are justified *if* their source is reliable.

Of course, no one thinks that crystal ball gazing is a reliable belief-forming process. But since we cannot step outside our minds to check for sure which sources are reliable and which are not, we must allow that the crystal ball gazer can ascribe the same conditional justificatory status to crystal ball gazing as we can to ordinary perception. Even though the externalist doesn't have to say that the crystal ball provides justification, they do still have to allow that *if* it is reliable it does, which is no less than what we can say of ordinary respectable evidential sources. So it would seem that buying into the Externalist Appeal to Reliability leaves us without grounds to reject various dodgy evidential sources and dodgy beliefs (Alston 1993, pg. 17 raises a similar concern).

As Lee points out, that this seems to make justification a matter of luck. Since we can't step outside our minds and check for sure which of our sources are actually

[24] Fumerton (1995, pp. 173-180), BonJour (1985) and Stroud (1989, pp. 47-48) express similar concerns. Fumerton points out that the externalist can sometimes have justified second-order beliefs about whether their first-order beliefs are actually justified, but only by justifying the reliability of their sources in a circular fashion. Since we are concerned to avoid circularity, that move is unavailable here.

reliable, it looks like we have to make do with our best guesses about which are and which aren't. If we are lucky, we will happen to trust reliable sources and hence happen to have justified beliefs. But having justification shouldn't be a matter of luck! The reason we have the concept of justification is to help us guide our beliefs: that is, to help us make principled decisions about what to believe and which sources to trust. A concept of justification that makes things simply a matter of luck fails to adequately serve the purpose of having a concept of justification in the first place.

A related point is that the Externalist Appeal to Reliability sits uneasily with our goal of forming true beliefs in such a manner as to avoid forming false ones. If we are content to rely on external facts to provide justification, then we are behaving in a manner which makes it less likely that we will achieve this goal. As I've pointed out, all manner of dodgy evidential sources could turn out to be reliable in fact, so conditional justification can actually be ascribed to all kinds of questionable beliefs. If we lack internally-accessible grounds for distinguishing between the justificatory states of different beliefs, then we risk believing in an unprincipled fashion. So paradoxically, the Externalist Appeal to Reliability actually makes it *less* likely that our internal belief-forming practices are reliable!

These are the reasons Lee offers against the Externalist Appeal to Reliability. I've tried to present them charitably and to provide some extra explanation, because I agree with the general sentiment and because Lee himself presents them only briefly. Now we can ask two questions: first, are they good reasons for rejecting the Appeal to Reliability? Second, do they also supply good objections to the Externalist Appeal to our Goal (which I outlined at the beginning of this Section)?

My own intuitions are mostly internalist, so I'm sympathetic to the reasons Lee offers against the Appeal to Reliability. However, I'm not sure that they sit so well with Lee's own argument. Notice that the bad company objection, the luck objection, and the tension between the Appeal to Reliability and our epistemic goal are all mostly just elaborations on the basic worry that trusting to the actual reliability of our sources means we can ascribe to them only conditional justificatory efficacy. This is because it seems that we cannot really ascertain whether our sources are reliable. But if Lee's own argument succeeds, then we can indeed have justification for the reliability of our sources, as I explained in Section 2.2. So the success of Lee's own argument would cause problems for his objections to the Appeal to Reliability, because it could turn out that even though we don't need justification for thinking our sources reliable, we have such justification anyway – and hence, can ascribe more than merely conditional justification to our beliefs.

Of course, that's only a problem for Lee if his own argument for accepting the reliability of our sources succeeds. And it remains to be seen whether it does succeed, because as I argued in Section 2.3, Lee's justifications for his first premise work out to be either too weak or circular. Since we haven't settled whether an alternative justification can be provided for the reasonability of our epistemic goal, a decisive verdict on his objections to the Appeal to Reliability can't be delivered just yet. However, it is worth noting that even if Lee's objections to it don't succeed, endorsing the Appeal to Reliability would mean denying [JR] and adopting a basic justification theory. I argued in Section 1.3 that all such theories allow bootstrapping, so it may turn out that the Bootstrapping Problem provides more reason for rejecting the Externalist Appeal to Reliability than Lee's objections do.

Our second question is whether Lee's objections to the Appeal to Reliability are also relevant to the Externalist Appeal to our Goal. I think they are more successful here, and that basically the same objections can motivate rejecting that proposal.

Lee's first premise is that it is reasonable to pursue our epistemic goal of forming true beliefs (in such a manner as to avoid forming false ones), and he thinks it is reasonable in part because true beliefs are necessary for making decisions relevant to our survival and moral obligations. I argued in Section 2.3 that Lee's claims about our survival and moral obligations are contingent empirical claims which can only be justified by appealing to our evidential sources, which threatens to make Lee's argument circular. But the Externalist Appeal to our Goal involves distinguishing between the truth of these claims and their justification. Presumably, in order for our moral obligations and survival interests to justify our evidential sources, it just has to be *true* that they make our epistemic goal reasonable, whether or not we also have justification for thinking that they do. So the suggestion is that Lee's argument works as long as the goal *is in fact* reasonable.

Like the Externalist Appeal to Reliability, the first worry with this approach is that it gives rise to a conditionality problem. Just as it looked like we could only say that our beliefs were 'justified *if* reliably caused', appealing to the reasonableness of our goal would mean saying that the reliability of our sources is 'justified *if* our goal is reasonable'. We can't step outside our own minds and check for sure whether we have moral obligations and survival interests that necessitate truth-seeking, so we cannot be sure that our goal is reasonable. Hence, if we accept the Externalist Appeal to our Goal, we must be happy to ascribe only conditional justificatory efficacy to our sources and hence only conditional justification to our beliefs. But surely we want more than that! Surely we want to know whether our sources actually provide justification, and whether our beliefs are actually justified. We should not rest content with only conditional justification. We should try to actually *show* that our goal is reasonable, and not just hope that it is.

As before, the conditionality problem gives rise to a bad company problem. If we can ascribe to our ordinary sources only a justificatory efficacy that is conditional upon the reasonableness of our goal, then we can ascribe to all manner of bogus sources a justificatory efficacy that is conditional upon the reasonableness of bogus goals. For instance, it may turn out (by cosmic chance) that our real interests are utterly unlike what we expect, so that the only genuinely reasonable epistemic goal is to support beliefs by coin-tossing. Hence, we can say that the method of confirming and disconfirming beliefs by tossing a coin provides us with justification that is conditional upon the reasonability of that goal. That's no different from saying that our evidential sources provide justification that is conditional upon the reasonability of truth seeking. But surely, we want to be able to maintain an internally-accessible distinction between sources that provide justification and those that don't. If we trust only to external facts to safeguard the justificatory efficacy of our sources, we cannot reliably distinguish genuine sources of justification from bogus ones.

Third, just as the Externalist Appeal to Reliability made gaining justification a matter of luck, so too does the Externalist Appeal to our Goal. The worry is that, if we lack internal means of determining which goals are reasonable and which sources best serve the pursuit of those goals, it would seem to be simply a matter of luck whether we end up trusting the sources which really do aid the pursuit of genuinely reasonable goals. But whether we are justified in believing things shouldn't be only a matter of luck: the concept of justification should actually be belief-guiding. So that is another reason to be dissatisfied with the Externalist Appeal to our Goal.

The idea that the concept of justification should be belief-guiding sits naturally with Lee's idea that justification is to be understood in terms of seeking truth in such a manner as to avoid error. If the nature and function of justification is to be explained with reference to this goal, then the externalist move would seem somewhat out of place. Conversely, if it were acceptable to appeal only to external facts to justify our beliefs, then it would seem that we would have little reason to really maintain a distinction between the concept of justification and the concept of truth in the first place: we might as well say that we are justified in believing claims if and only if they are true. The fact that we maintain this distinction reflects the fact that we cannot rely only on external facts: even if truth is what we're after, the fact that we cannot always access truth directly means that we have developed the concept of justification to use as an approximation. Justification is a matter of internally accessible reasons.

A related point is that the Externalist Appeal to our Goal works out to be self-defeating. The idea is that, if moral or prudential considerations do make it the case that we ought to pursue truth (in such a manner as to avoid error), then this is a reasonable goal for us to have. But trusting only to external facts to justify our beliefs (including facts about the reasonableness of our goals) would actually make us less likely to achieve this goal, compared to trying to support our beliefs by internally accessible reasons. This is because being content with merely conditional ascriptions of justification would mean giving up on being able to tell the difference between trustworthy and untrustworthy sources, which would threaten our ability to actually form true beliefs in such a manner as to also avoid error. Consequently, if our epistemic goal is in fact reasonable, as the externalist hopes, then we in fact have a reason not to be satisfied with the externalist's proposal. The Externalist Appeal to our Goal is self-defeating.

In this Section I've considered the prospects for an externalist modification to Lee's approach, which tries to justify his first premise by trusting solely to the fact that our epistemic goal is reasonable whether or not we are justified in thinking that it is. Even if the fact that our goal is reasonable really does justify our sources, I've argued that we shouldn't be satisfied with merely hoping that this is the case. I have argued this by appealing to reasons resembling ones that Lee himself offers against a very similar externalist strategy. These objections are probably no absolutely decisive, so externalists might still be satisfied with the appeal to our goal even we cannot say for sure whether our beliefs are justified. However, my view is that we ought not to give up on trying to find an internally-accessible justification for our epistemic goal. Accordingly, I will develop an internalist modification to Lee's approach in the next two Sections.

3.2 An Internalist Approach

Another kind of justification for the goal is this. Whether or not our moral obligations and interests in survival make the pursuit of truth reasonable, it is surely the case that we would prefer to have true beliefs about the world. This gives us a reason to accept those sources that are most likely to help us get at the truth, even if their reliability is not guaranteed absolutely. Of course, we do have to ask whether our preference is reasonable. But the reasonableness of a preference is a matter of its compatibility with other preferences, and by and large the preference for truth doesn't conflict with our other preferences. So the status of our epistemic goal as a reasonable preference means that Lee's first premise can be justified on internally-accessible grounds.

Let me explain this approach a little further. The basic idea is that we simply have a *preference* for forming true beliefs (in such a manner as to also avoid error), and since our preferences are internally-accessible, we have an internally-accessible reason for thinking that we should accept the reliability of our evidential sources. Whether or not accepting them is *also* made reasonable by external facts, I argued in Section 3.1 that it is desirable to also have internally-accessible reasons for accepting the reliability of our sources because we should want to be able to ascribe more than merely conditional justification to our beliefs. So this is an internalist modification on Lee's argument which should meet that requirement.

Of course, this response is only going to be satisfactory to someone who really does prefer true beliefs. In addition, I pointed out in Section 2.3 that the kind of truth-seeking we need to make Lee's argument work isn't the kind of truth-seeking that forms the absolute minimum basis for rational inquiry. In order to inquire rationally about things, you don't necessarily need to care for having true beliefs about the world, you only need to care for having true beliefs about what to believe. Hence, the response I suggest will only be acceptable to those who want to pursue truth (in such a manner as to avoid error) with respect to the external world.

I for one do have this preference, and I will assume that most other people do too. But I am happy to concede that this response won't persuade the sceptic who doesn't care for true beliefs about the external world, whom I considered in Section 2.3. The point of this proposal isn't to persuade sceptics: it is to explain why we, ordinary non-sceptics who do care about having true beliefs, are justified in accepting the reliability of our evidential sources in a manner which avoids epistemic circularity.

Of course, we still have to consider whether our preference is actually reasonable. Notice that the first premise in Lee's argument is the claim that it is reasonable for us to pursue our epistemic goal, and so the argument would fail if it turned out that our preference for truth-seeking actually turned out to be unreasonable.

My view is that the only way to evaluate the reasonableness of a preference is on the basis of other preferences. By themselves, preferences are reasonable by default, and so taken in isolation they are immune to rational criticism. As Hume says, 'We speak not strictly and philosophically when we talk of the combat of passion and of reason. Reason is, and ought only to be the slave of the passions, and can never pretend to any other office than to serve and obey them.' (Hume 1739-40:1978. 3:2:3. pg. 415). I interpret what Hume calls 'passions' to be the same as thing as preferences, and so I take the Humean line that there is nothing more to the question of whether a preference is reasonable than the question of whether it is in conflict with other preferences.

Does our preference for (principled) truth-seeking conflict with our other preferences? This will obviously depend upon individual cases, and it isn't impossible that there could be inquirers for whom there is a conflict. For instance, we can probably imagine an epistemically paranoid inquirer who worries so greatly about avoiding having false beliefs that they are not prepared to risk taking a chance on our evidential sources at all. William James (1896:1962. pg. 50) describes this type of inquirer as being 'like a general informing his soldiers that it is better to keep out of battle forever than to risk a single wound.' I am prepared to admit that a thinker like this won't be satisfied with the internalist response I propose here, because for them the search for truth won't be reasonable, as long as there is a stronger preference in place for avoiding error. But I think that for most of us, for the most part, the preference for truth does not conflict significantly with other preferences.

Of course, we can still admit a few exceptions even for regular inquirers. I am still making background use of a pragmatic view of justification which allows that other preferences besides truth-seeking can sometimes justify beliefs. In certain cases, these preferences will override the preference for truth by making it the case that you ought to believe something for which you have insufficient or contrary evidence. For instance, in Section 2.1 I considered a case in which you form the belief 'I will survive this illness' because it will increase your chances of survival, even though you have evidence that in fact you probably won't survive.

These are exceptions to the general rule. By and large, I think it likely that the preference for truth doesn't conflict, in matters of belief, with other preferences. In fact, if we have any preferences that require us to make decisions about how to act in the world, then it looks like we need accurate information relevant to making those decisions. For instance, if I want to know which graduate school to go to, I will need accurate information about the merits of the various programmes. So the reasonableness of my preference for seeking truth is actually increased by my other preference for going to a good grad school. By and large, I think that most of our preferences are externally-directed preferences that require action in the world, and so they will make our preference for truth-seeking even more reasonable because choosing how to act requires having good information.

One objection to my view would be that it rests upon a substantive and broadly Humean account of the reasonability of preferences, and I haven't provided much independent motivation for that account. My chief concern in this thesis is epistemic circularity, and so to avoid going too far afield I won't be able to develop a detailed argument for the Humean view of preferences that I'm working with. A fully comprehensive version of the internalist response I have proposed would obviously have to support the Humean view of preferences in more detail. However, I do find this account to have sufficient independent plausibility for present purposes, and it may turn out that its advantages in helping us to avoid circularity provide extra reason to accept it. Nonetheless, I will briefly consider one objection to the account.

Although I think that the reasonability of our preferences can only be assessed on the basis of other preferences, you might think that our preferences are susceptible to moral evaluation as well. That is, it may be possible to ask whether my preference for eating these chocolates is morally reasonable, given that the chocolates belong to you, and you haven't granted me permission to eat them. If our moral obligations override our preferences, then it would seem that we have a basis for rationally evaluating our preferences which does not derive from other preferences.

I argued in Section 2.3 that the existence of beings to whom we could have moral obligations is an empirical claim which depends upon the use of our sources, so we can't assume from the outset that we have any such obligations. But even if we do, the reasonability of our epistemic goal is hardly vitiated. The existence of overriding moral obligations would make our epistemic goal *more* justified, because seeking truth is necessary if we are to make principled decisions about how to act morally in the world. So we can say that our goal is reasonable on the basis of our internally-accessible preferences, and potentially also reasonable on the basis of external moral facts. The point is that we shouldn't rely only on the external facts.

What I've suggested is an internalist modification on Lee's basic argument. So, for the justification of perception, we get the same argument as before; except that this time the justification for premise [1] comes from the fact that (principled) truth-seeking is a reasonable preference:

1. It is reasonable for us to pursue the epistemic goal. [Premise]
2. The best means of bringing about the epistemic goal requires accepting the general reliability of our perceptual judgments. [Premise]
3. ∴ It is reasonable for us to accept the general reliability of our perceptual judgments. [1, 2]

[Lee 2014, pg. 422; adapted very slightly]

As before, the justification for premise [2] just comes from the fact that assuming our perceptual judgements to be reliable is the most coherent explanation for our experiences, and hence the one that is most likely to be true as far as we can tell.

We just about have a successful pragmatic response to the Problem of the Criterion, and hence to the Argument from Evidential Circularity. The response involves affirming [JR] with respect to our evidential sources, but denying that you can only justify their reliability by evidence. Instead, we can say that claims affirming their reliability are justified on account of the relationship between our evidential sources and our epistemic goal, and that the goal is justified because it is a rational preference.

There are two more problems we need to look at before this response can be considered complete. In Section 3.3 I will examine a remaining problem for the internalist pragmatic approach I have suggested, then in Chapter Four I will raise a new problem for the pragmatic view of justification in general. I will develop solutions to both of them.

3.3 Introspective Circularity

One worry I have with the internalist proposal is that it isn't yet completely free of epistemic circularity. Lee's main example of an evidential source is perception, and so his argument is framed accordingly. However, he claims (pg. 430) that the same kind of argument can be used to justify accepting the reliability of introspection (and that of memory). I think the claim about introspection commits him to the following inference:

1. It is reasonable for us to pursue the epistemic goal. [Premise]
2. The best means of bringing about the epistemic goal requires accepting the general reliability of our introspective judgments. [Premise]
3. ∴ It is reasonable for us to accept the general reliability of our introspective judgments. [1, 2]

In Section 2.3 I argued that Lee's original justification for premise [1] failed, but in Section 3.2 I developed an alternative justification for it which treats our epistemic goal as an internally-accessible preference which as reasonable by default. But whether or not you have a particular preference is a contingent psychological fact, of the kind that can only be accessed by introspection. So it would seem that we have a situation whereby introspection justifies a premise in an argument for accepting its own reliability – and hence, its own justificatory efficacy. This means that an appeal to our preferences in trying to salvage Lee's argument won't yet help us to avoid epistemic circularity.

Of course, the kind of circularity here isn't exactly inferential in character, because the conclusion of [1-3] isn't that introspection is a source of justification, but only that it is reasonable for us to accept its general reliability. Nonetheless, I pointed out in Section 2.2 that if the argument succeeds, we ought to form the belief 'introspection is reliable' as a result. So we can say that the argument provides non-inferential justification for that claim. Having justification for a claim affirming the reliability of a source means having justification for a claim affirming its justificatory efficacy, so if introspection is used to support premise [1], it is implicated in an instance of non-inferential epistemically circular justification.

This circumstance also spells trouble for Lee's approach in general. Presumably, we can offer an argument like [1-3] in support of any evidential source which stands the best chance of delivering truths about a particular domain, as long as we care about having true beliefs with respect to that domain. But all arguments of that form will feature a premise affirming the reasonableness of our goal, and I've argued that its reasonability derives from its being a preference. Since our preferences are only accessible by introspection, all arguments of the form [1-3] will rely on the justificatory efficacy of introspection. But justifying introspection itself using such an argument would be circular, and our current project is to avoid circular justification. So unless introspection can be justified on non-pragmatic grounds, no argument of the form [1-3] will justify accepting the reliability of an evidential source.

In my view, the way to resolve this problem is to challenge the idea that introspection stands in the same need of justification as ordinary evidential sources. The traditional view in epistemology is that we have privileged access to our own mental states: as much as we can doubt whether our thoughts about the world are correct, it seems impossible to doubt *that* we think what we do. Even if I can doubt whether I have hands, for instance, I cannot doubt that I *believe* that I have hands, or that I would *prefer* to have hands. Introspective judgements just don't seem open to doubt in quite the same way as, say, visual judgements.

Notice also that introspection was not amongst the evidential sources that we originally considered when we looked at the Problem of the Criterion in Section 1.2, and particularly when we considered the idea that you can only justify a source's reliability by evidence. For instance, recall James Van Cleve's concern about justifying the reliability of our perceptual faculties:

> Principles affirming the reliability of our faculties are both *contingent* and *general*. For me, it is hard to see how a principle combining these features can be basic – at least if basic propositions comprise only those that are somehow immediately evident or obvious. [Van Cleve 2003, pg. 51]

We might think that this is a perfectly reasonable concern to have about a source like vision, or hearing, or memory. But the reliability of introspection looks like quite a different story. I can be a lot surer about my mental states than I can about my perceptions. Even to say justifiably that I doubt whether introspection is reliable would be to assume that I have reliable introspective access to my doubts. Since doubting is a contingent psychological state, it would seem there is something self-contradictory about saying that I doubt my introspective access to those states. So we might be tempted to take up the traditional opinion that introspection is justified *a priori*.

I think there are two different ways of making this idea more precise. The first proposal would be to accept [JR] as a principle which applies to our regular evidential sources – that is, vision, memory, hearing and the like, whose evidential domain is external to our own present mental states – but deny that [JR] applies to introspection. The idea would be that we have a default entitlement to our particular introspective judgements, even if we don't know that they are generally reliable, but that the reliability of any *other* source needs to be confirmed before it can provide justification.

But this proposal isn't the best way to make sense of the idea that we have privileged access to our mental states. The reason it is faulty is that it would expose us to the Bootstrapping Problem, whereby you could just use your introspective judgements to confirm their own reliability in the manner I described in Section 1.3. Since bootstrapping is an epistemically circular procedure, this particular proposal won't help our attempt at a response to the Argument from Evidential Circularity.

A second proposal is to maintain that [JR] applies to introspection, just as it does to any evidential source, but to hold that we have a default entitlement to think our introspective judgements reliable. This would prevent our being able to gain justification by bootstrapping, because our prior justification for thinking introspection reliable will constrain the strength of the inductive evidence that we can gain from it. (I described this constraint in Section 1.3; and it has been formally modelled by Barnett 2014).

I think this second proposal succeeds. [JR] is a requirement that applies to all our evidential sources, but the requirement is met automatically in the case of introspection, and met via Lee's pragmatic argument in the case of our other sources. An internally-accessible justification for Lee's first premise is provided by the fact that seeking truth is a reasonable preference, and we have introspective access to our preferences. Since the reliability of introspection is justified *a priori*, not via a pragmatic argument, we have an explanation for the justificatory efficacy of our evidential sources which doesn't involve epistemic circularity. This means we have a response to the Argument from

Evidential Circularity. We can endorse a pragmatic account of justification and deny premise [4] in the Argument.

How plausible is it that the reliability of introspection is justified *a priori*? I think this view is quite plausible, though admittedly it has come under a little more scrutiny recently.[25] A fully comprehensive response to the Argument from Evidential Circularity along the lines I have suggested would have to go into the epistemology of introspection in more detail, and since my main concern here is with epistemic circularity, I'll try to avoid straying too far afield. Nonetheless, I will say a little more in favour of thinking that the reliability of introspection is justified *a priori*. I'm not sure if this extra consideration is absolutely decisive, but it may be a good target for further investigation.

One reason for thinking that we have a default entitlement to introspection's reliability borrows Lee's appeal to the presuppositions of rational inquiry. His idea was that the reasonability of (principled) truth-seeking was a minimum presupposition for rationally inquiring after anything. I argued in Section 2.3 that this insight, even if correct, is still too weak to provide any support for his first premise. But I think we can say that the reliability of introspection is a rational presupposition in a more substantial sense. The idea is that rational inquiry (and by extension, rational discourse) is a process of forming beliefs, subjecting some beliefs to doubt, accepting others with confidence, examining reasons for belief, and the like. This requires some access to its subject matter. If we cannot assume that we have justified introspective access to what we believe, what we doubt, what our internal grounds for belief are, what we accept and what we reject, then we cannot rationally engage in this process.

[25] See Schwitzgebel (2011a, 2011b).

Of course, what we need to establish in order for this response to work is that we have justified introspective access to our preferences in particular, since the point is to show that we can support Lee's first premise by identifying our goal as an internally accessible preference. But I think we can establish this as a rational presupposition also. The idea is that inquiry is not an unmotivated task: we are interested in particular questions for particular reasons. Our preferences form the motivations for asking certain questions and the standards for evaluating prospective answers.

Unless we assume that we have justified introspective access to our preferences, we cannot engage rationally in any kind of motivated inquiry. But if we can have introspective access to our preferences regarding inquiry, then we can have introspective access to our preference for inquiry after true beliefs about the world. So unlike the epistemic goal itself, the efficacy of introspection (by which we can access a preference for that goal) is a rational presupposition in the right kind of way.

Of course, the presupposition is only that introspection has justificatory efficacy, and what we need to show is that we have a default entitlement to its reliability, which is slightly different. But we can establish this very easily. Given that we have had to affirm [JR] in the course of providing a pragmatic response to the Argument from Evidential Circularity, and given that [JR] is just the claim that the justificatory efficacy of a source entails justification for thinking it reliable, we can say that its reliability is hence a presupposition of rational inquiry as well. So we have *a priori* justification for thinking introspection reliable.

This extra consideration might not be completely decisive. In my view, the idea that we have *a priori* justification for introspection's reliability is already sufficiently plausible from the outset, partly because it isn't possible to doubt its reliability without assuming reliable introspective access to our doubts. However, I am aware that a fully detailed version of account I have proposed would need to address the epistemology of introspection in more detail, so I have suggested what think is a good target for future investigation. What I hope to have established is that the Argument from Evidential Circularity shouldn't persuade anyone tempted to take up the traditional view that we have a default entitlement to the reliability of introspection.

In addition, nothing I've said should suggest we can assume that introspection is *perfectly* reliable. The idea is only that we have *a priori* justification to believe that introspection is sufficiently reliable to justify its outputs, including the claim that we have a preference for (principled) truth-seeking.

To recap. In Chapter One I formulated the Argument from Evidential Circularity, which tries to show that epistemically circular justification is possible. In Chapter Two I considered the prospects for responding to it by recourse to pragmatism about justification, and I presented an existing pragmatic argument developed by Byeong Lee (2013), which appeals to our epistemic goal. I tried to show that Lee's account had some flaws, and in this Chapter I've tried to rectify those by considering an externalist and an internalist modification to his original proposal.

In Section 3.1 I argued that we shouldn't rely solely on external facts to justify our epistemic goal, and so I've tried to provide internally-accessible grounds for thinking that this goal is reasonable. In Section 3.2 I proposed that we have a preference for seeking truth, and the preference is reasonable because it doesn't generally clash with our other preferences. We can come to know whether we have this preference by introspection, and in Section 3.3 I argued that introspection has a special evidential status because its reliability is justified *a priori*. The reliability of our other sources can be established via a series of pragmatic arguments (of the same form as Lee's) based on the idea that each fundamental evidential source stands the best chance of delivering truth with respect to its particular domain. This means that we can affirm [JR], but avoid the Argument from Evidential Circularity by denying its fourth premise.

Chapter Four: Bootstrapping for Pragmatists

The response I have developed in the previous Chapter is a pragmatic one. Pragmatism about justification is the view that beliefs can be justified on the basis of your goals, preferences and interests. But whatever its advantages in helping us to avoid the Argument from Evidential Circularity, I worry that pragmatism faces a closely related problem. I will address that problem in this Chapter. In Section 4.1 I will show that pragmatism seems to license bootstrapping procedures similar to the ones I discussed in Section 1.3. The idea is that you can use your pragmatically-justified beliefs to show that your pragmatic reasoning is a source of *evidential* justification as well. In Section 4.2 I'll propose some modifications to the pragmatist view, which will enable us to avoid this problem.

4.1 Bootstrapping with Prudential Reasoning

One of the examples I used to motivate pragmatism back in Section 2.1 was a case in which you are in hospital with a terrible illness (the example is adapted from Reisner 2008, pg. 25). You know that you have only a 10% chance of survival, but you can double this chance if you form the belief 'I will survive this illness'. Of course, it is unlikely that your belief will be correct, for you will still have only a 20% chance of survival once you believe it. But it looks like you are justified in believing it anyway. The idea is that your prudential interest in surviving overrides whatever evidence you have against your belief.

Let's consider what kind of reasoning you might carry out in a situation like this. I think the reasoning would look like the following:

1. I am prudentially justified in trying to survive this illness. [Premise]

2. The best means of bringing it about that I will survive this illness is to believe 'I will survive this illness'. [Premise]

3. ∴ I am prudentially justified in believing 'I will survive this illness'. [1, 2]

This type of reasoning is a perfectly straightforward example of practical reasoning from ends to means. Notice that the conclusion is not that you will survive this illness, but only that you prudentially ought to believe you will. Acting on your reasoning requires following through on that conclusion, and actually believing what you prudentially ought to. Accordingly, let us suppose you form the belief:

4. I will survive this illness. [Premise]

Of course, [4] is not an inferential consequence of the reasoning from [1-3]: you don't infer [4] as a conclusion. Instead it is a kind of causal consequence, just as ordinary physical actions are the causal consequences of deliberation. But just as ordinary prudential reasoning can show which physical actions are justified, [1-3] purports to show that [4] is a justified belief. So [4] itself counts as a non-inferentially justified belief, just like the kind a basic justification theorist thinks you can have.

So now you believe 'I am prudentially justified in believing 'I will survive this illness'', and you believe 'I will survive this illness'. This puts you in a position to infer a surprising conclusion. Since any proposition is logically equivalent to a claim affirming that that proposition is correct, you can now infer:

5. ∴ 'I will survive this illness' is correct. [4]

6. ∴ What I am prudentially justified in believing is correct (in this instance).[3,5]

This is a surprising result, for obviously the evidence makes it likely that you are *not* believing correctly. Remember that even once you believe [4], you still have only a 20% chance of survival. Yet by deducing the logically equivalent proposition [5], and putting it together with [3], you can purport to show that your prudential interests are not leading you to form a false belief after all.

But the trouble doesn't stop there. As with regular bootstrapping, it is easy to apply this type of reasoning broadly. Doing so will allow the following inference:

7. [conclusions derived from many more inferences of the form 1-6] [Premises]

8. ∴ Whenever I am prudentially justified in believing a claim, that claim is correct. [Induction from 6, 7]

9. My evidence for a claim is just whatever increases my epistemic likelihood that the claim is correct. [Premise]

10. ∴ My prudential reasoning is a source of evidence. [8, 9]

As with the example of bootstrapping I used in Section 1.3, premise [7] is a stand-in for a large number of other instances in which you repeat the same reasoning as [1-6], though about a different proposition each time. By doing this, you can end up with many justified conclusions to the effect that what you are prudentially justified in believing is correct in each case. From these you can inductively establish that whenever you are prudentially justified in believing something, it is correct. Your evidence for a claim is just whatever makes it more 'epistemically likely' for you that the claim is true – that is, more likely from your point of view, given the information you have available. So it follows that your prudential reasoning about particular claims actually is a source of evidence about those claims.

I take it that this consequence is an embarrassment to pragmatism! The idea that prudential reasoning is a source of *evidence* looks very suspicious. The whole point of pragmatism about justification is the idea that your goals and preferences can make you justified in believing claims, even when the evidence is insufficient.

Of course, it may turn out that prudential reasoning is ultimately what gives us justification for trusting our evidential sources. In the previous two Chapters we looked at Byeong Lee's argument to this effect, and I proposed some modifications which I think make Lee's approach more plausible. If the best reasons we have for trusting our evidential sources are prudential reasons, then it might seem like there is a certain sense in which prudential reasoning is a source of evidence. It provides an explanation for how we can gain justification from sources like vision, hearing, or memory. Our evidential justification is ultimately grounded in prudential justification.

But that's not the sense in which we are meant to interpret [10]. The idea with [10] is not that prudential reasoning *supports* evidential sources, but that prudential reasoning is *itself* an evidential source. The idea is that whenever you are prudentially justified in believing a claim, that claim is correct. And this idea looks very fishy indeed.

It's also possible to construct bootstrap-style inferences which show that prudential reasoning is a source of evidence about very specific domains. To illustrate, imagine that you are an athlete trying to psych yourself up for a big race (you may recall this example from Section 2.1). You know that you can increase your chances of winning by believing that you will win. In addition, suppose that you have 99 more races scheduled, and that the best way to increase your chances of winning *this* race is to believe that you will win each of those as well. Hence, you have prudential justification for each of a series of beliefs: 'I will win race 1', 'I will win race 2', 'I will win race 3'… and so on. Furthermore, suppose that you have evidence that you will actually not win any of these races. For instance, suppose that you regularly compete against athletes who are much better than you are. So each of your 100 beliefs *right now* about your future performance is justified in spite of the evidence.

This puts you in a position to bootstrap in the same fashion as [1-10]. By working out that you ought to believe each of the 100 claims about your future performance, and by actually believing them, you can work out that what you are prudentially justified in believing is correct in each of 100 cases. These cases are cases of a special kind: cases of belief about your athletic ability in spite of contrary evidence. This gives you inductive grounds for thinking that whenever you are prudentially justified in believing that you'll win a race in spite of the evidence, you will win. And you'll be able to infer from this that prudential reasoning is a source of evidence about a very particular type of situation: namely whether you will win against athletes more capable than yourself, in situations where your other evidence indicates that you won't win. Even if your original 100 beliefs about your performance are justified, this higher-order belief about your prudential reasoning doesn't seem justified. So the worry is that bootstrap-style reasoning allows you to justify problematic conclusions in a problematic fashion.

As I see it, the possibility of inferences like [1-10] is an embarrassment to pragmatism, whether the conclusion is very general (like [10]) or very specific (like the athletic example). Unless it is possible to modify the pragmatist theory, I think this problem seriously detracts from its plausibility. So this is a significant challenge to the prospects for a pragmatic response to the Argument from Evidential Circularity along the lines I have suggested.

Is bootstrapping for pragmatists, like bootstrapping for basic justification theorists, an instance of epistemic circularity? That depends. In Section 1.1 I defined an epistemically circular justificatory structure as one in which a justification source S provides you with justification for the claim 'S is a justification source'. This is a variant of a more general type of structure concerning any epistemically valuable property ε (such as knowledge, justification, warrant, rational acceptability, and the like), whereby an ε-source S provides you with ε for the claim 'S is an ε-source'. Let's consider whether bootstrapping for pragmatists is an instance of this kind of structure insofar as it applies to justification.

The conclusion of the argument [1-10] is that your prudential reasoning is a source of evidence, which means that it is a source of justification. Of course, the pragmatist obviously agreed already that prudential reasoning is a source of justification. But what they agreed to was that prudential reasoning is a source of prudential justification, not a source of evidential justification. That is, they agreed that prudential considerations can justify beliefs without making it more likely that those beliefs are true. But by starting with prudential justification, and by engaging in the procedure [1-10], it looks like we have been able to show that prudential reasoning does provide evidence as well. So [1-10] is an instance of a justificatory structure whereby prudential reasoning provides prudential justification for the claim that it is a source of evidential justification.

This means that [1-10] is close to being epistemically circular, but is not quite. The definition of epistemic circularity I have provided is only an instance of a general pattern whereby source S provides ε for the claim 'S is an ε-source', and it looks like ε could stand for either prudential justification or evidential justification, but not both. So the problem is closely related to epistemic circularity, but is actually a non-circular version of the Bootstrapping Problem which is distinctive to pragmatism.

4.2 Attention and Closure

I've tried to show that pragmatism about justified belief allows you to infer problematic conclusions from justified premises, via a procedure very similar to bootstrapping. This threatens the plausibility of a pragmatic response to the Argument from Evidential Circularity. So what I'll do in this Section is propose a modification to the basic pragmatist theory, in order to disallow this procedure.

One easy response to the Bootstrapping Problem is unavailable to the pragmatist. As I pointed out in Section 1.3, theories which endorse [JR] don't license bootstrapping because [JR] prevents you being able to use a source to amplify your justification for its reliability. So any source with respect to which [JR] is true cannot be implicated in a bootstrapping procedure. The account I have developed in Chapter Three for avoiding evidential circularity involves affirming [JR] with respect to our fundamental evidential sources.

But though I think [JR] applies to our evidential sources, it is implausible that it applies to our prudential reasoning. That is, it's implausible that you need justification to think it evidentially reliable in order for it to provide prudential justification. What's important about pragmatism is that it allows reasons for belief that are not evidential. In addition, the problem with bootstrapping for pragmatists isn't just the means by which you gain justification for [10], but the implausibility of [10] itself. If [JR] were true with respect to prudential reasoning, then justification for [10] would be a precondition for its justificatory efficacy, which would hardly avoid the problem. So it wouldn't be desirable for the pragmatist to affirm [JR] with respect to our prudential reasoning.

I think the right way to disallow bootstrapping for pragmatists is to constrain the use of prudentially justified beliefs in deductive reasoning. Notice that a crucial step in the argument I presented last Section was the following:

3. I am prudentially justified in believing 'I will survive this illness'. [1, 2]

4. I will survive this illness. [Premise]

5. ∴ 'I will survive this illness' is correct. [4]

6. ∴ What I am prudentially justified in believing is correct (in this instance). [3, 5]

My proposal is that you cannot justifiably infer [6], because you cannot justifiably direct your attention to both [3] and [5] at the same time as long as [5] is supported solely by prudential considerations. Ultimately this prevents you from bootstrapping to any dodgy claims about the evidential status of your prudential reasoning.

Let me explain my proposal by pointing out the distinction between believing a claim and consciously attending to it. Right you probably believe the claim 'Wellington is the capital of New Zealand', and now that I have mentioned the proposition you are probably paying conscious attention to it. But presumably you believed 'Wellington is the capital of New Zealand' even before I directed your attention to it. So there is a difference between believing a claim and attending to it. We believe a great number of claims simultaneously, but at any given time only a tiny fraction of what we believe is the object of conscious attention. The vast majority of our beliefs are held 'in the background'.

Let's see how we can use this distinction to inform a judgement about the inference [1-6]. In our example, your epistemic situation is characterised by four main beliefs:

[3] 'I am prudentially justified in believing 'I will survive this illness''

[3*] 'I am not evidentially justified in believing 'I will survive this illness''

[4] 'I will survive this illness'

[5] ''I will survive this illness' is correct.'

Of course, [3*] wasn't a belief that featured in your initial prudential reasoning or in your subsequent bootstrapping inference. But [3*] is a background belief that describes an important feature of your situation. What's important in the hospital example is that you are prudentially justified in believing that you will survive, but not evidentially justified – which the pragmatist needs in order to show that prudential considerations can override evidential ones. The bootstrapping procedure is surprising in part because you shouldn't be able to infer that what you prudentially ought to believe is correct as long as [3*] is true.

I think the distinction between belief and attention is relevant to what you can do with these four beliefs. My proposal is that there are norms governing what you can justifiably direct your attention to, just as there are norms governing what you can justifiably believe. And just as your prudential interests can influence what you are justified in believing, they can influence what you are justified in attending to.

So I allow that you can justifiably believe all four at the same time, but I deny that you can justifiably direct your conscious attention to certain combinations of them. I think that you cannot justifiably direct your attention to either of [3] or [3*] at the same time as either of [4] or [5]. Any combination involving one of the first two and one of the second two is rationally prohibited.

This constraint is plausible because being aware that you only believe something for prudential reasons (and not for evidential ones) is likely to make believing it more difficult. As Marušić (2011) worries, it might be that 'one cannot deliberately believe something on the basis of nonevidential reasons, that is, *in full awareness* that these are one's reasons' (pg. 35, italics added). I argued in Section 2.1 that pragmatism doesn't necessarily assume that you can exercise voluntary control over your beliefs. That is, what you prudentially ought to believe could just be what you ought to *get yourself* to believe. But getting yourself to believe something can involve ignoring certain other beliefs. And even if you don't have direct voluntary control over your beliefs, it's likely that you do have voluntary control over your attention. So part of getting yourself to believe [4] will be to voluntarily ignore [3] and [3*], even if you still do believe them.

So my proposal is that pragmatism ought to be understood as a theory of what you are justified in consciously attending to, as well as a theory of what you are justified in believing. The resources by which the pragmatist can explain what you are justified in consciously attending to are the same as those by which they explain what you are justified in believing, because attention plays a role in making certain things easier to believe. As with belief, what you are justified in attending to depends in part upon your goals and preferences.

The justification of attention hasn't been examined as much as the justification of belief. My suspicion is that some problems which look like they concern justified belief – such as bootstrapping for pragmatists – are really problems concerning justified attention. A more comprehensive discussion of the problem of bootstrapping for pragmatists would have to provide a lot more detail about the prospects for developing a theory for justified attention, which I won't try to do here. Here I will just say a few things to try to make my view more plausible.

To some extent, my proposal borrows elements of contextualism about justified belief and applies these to attention. Contextualism about justified belief is the view that what you are justified in believing depends in part upon your context.[26] Accordingly, we can say that contextualism about justified attention would be the view that what you are justified in paying attention to depends in part upon your context.

When we try to work out what we are prudentially justified in believing, we are in a special context: the context of reasoning prudentially about belief. And it is appropriate to consciously attend to beliefs like [3] and [3*] in that context. However, when it comes to actually maintaining optimistic beliefs in the face of contrary evidence, we leave the context of prudential reasoning and enter the context of optimistic belief. What we ought to focus on in that context are not claims *about* what we prudentially ought to believe, but the *content* of what we ought to believe. When you're trying to maintain your belief in [4], you shouldn't be thinking about [3] or [3*]. Once you've worked that you are prudentially justified in believing [4], you should just focus on [4]. So what you are justified in consciously attending to is determined in part by your context, which is determined in part by your goals.

Notice that I'm not saying that you ought to actually disbelieve or suspend judgement about claims you are not justified in attending to. You can still justifiably believe each of the four claims I have been discussing, only you cannot direct your attention to certain combinations of them. You cannot attend to [4] and [5] in the context of prudential reasoning about what to believe, and you cannot attend to [3] and [3*] in the context of optimistic belief.

[26] There are also versions which relativise the appropriateness of knowledge and justification attributions to the context of the attributor rather than of the subject. See DeRose (1999) for discussion.

The upshot of my proposal is that you cannot justifiably construct an argument which features [3] and [5] as premises, at least as long as you lack sufficient evidence that you will survive. Because the attentional contexts of each belief differ, such that you are not justified in considering them both at the same time, you cannot confirm that what you prudentially ought to believe is actually correct. That is, as long as [3*] is true, the different attentional contexts of [3] and [5] prevent you from being able to legitimately infer [6].

The same constraint applies to any instance in which you have prudential but not evidential justification to believe something. This means that no inference of the same type as [3-6] will be legitimate, and so you won't be able to amass the kind of evidence that you need in order to bootstrap. That is, unless you have independent evidence that what you prudentially ought to believe is correct, you won't be able to justify a set of claims affirming that it is. The result is that the sort of procedure I described in Section 4.1 cannot justify the claim that your prudential reasoning is a source of evidence, at least if we accept the modifications to pragmatism that I have proposed.

Of course, things would be a bit different if you did have evidence for the claim 'I will survive this illness'. Then you could justifiably attend to [3] and [5] at the same time, and hence you could infer that what you are prudentially justified in believing is correct. But that's only permissible if you have independent evidence that you will survive – that is, only if [3*] is false. This is because your beliefs about your survival would no longer be cases of optimism in the face of difficulty, and so would no longer be held in an attentional context that must be kept separate from the context of prudential reasoning. In that circumstance there would be no rational prohibition on your ability to confirm that what you are prudentially justified in believing is correct.

I have suggested a modification to the basic pragmatist theory of justified belief. My view is that the same prudential considerations that can justify beliefs can also make it the case that you are or are not justified in paying conscious attention to various combinations of beliefs. Obviously a fully worked out version of this proposal would have to go into a lot more detail, but take what I've said as proof of concept. The idea is that we can disallow the bootstrappish reasoning I outlined in Section 4.1 by limiting how you can use certain beliefs in the course of deductive reasoning.

The result of my proposal is that the argument outlined in Section 4.1 cannot provide you with doxastic justification. That is, you cannot come to have a justified belief in its conclusion. But we might worry that it could still provide you with propositional justification. As I pointed out in Section 1.1, propositional justification is the kind of justification you can have for a claim, whether or not you believe it. And even having propositional justification for the conclusion of a bootstrapping argument would be an embarrassment to the pragmatist view.

I think my proposal avoids this consequence as well. In my view, doxastic justification is the primary notion with respect to which propositional justification ought to be understood. The idea is that propositional justification is a kind of counterfactual extension of doxastic justification: what you have propositional justification to believe is just what you would have doxastic justification to believe, were you to form the relevant beliefs. So if there is an inferential procedure that can never provide you with doxastic justification – like bootstrapping for pragmatists – then the inferential structure can never provide you with propositional justification either.

Accepting this view means denying that propositional justification is closed under deductive entailment. That is, it means denying the following principle:

[CPJ]: If you have propositional justification for premises [p1-p*n*], and [p1-p*n*] deductively entail conclusion [Q], then you have propositional justification for [Q].[27]

[CPJ] is a plausible principle, so denying it might look a bit ad hoc. It might look like I'm only denying [CPJ] in order to disallow bootstrapping. But I don't think it should be so surprising that a pragmatist ought to deny [CPJ]. Whenever you maintain a prudentially justified belief in the face of evidence, you lack justification for the claim that your prudentially justified belief is wrong – even though your evidence makes that claim likely. Although this doesn't amount to the denial of [CPJ], the idea is that even an unmodified version of pragmatism ought to restrict propositional justification in a manner which is not far from denying [CPJ].

Consider the hospital example. In the example, you are justified in believing 'I will survive this illness', but your evidence makes it likely that you won't. Even without the modifications I've proposed, the pragmatist ought to deny that your evidence gives you propositional justification for the claim 'I won't survive this illness'. This restriction doesn't amount to a denial of [CPJ], because your evidence doesn't deductively entail that you won't survive, but it does amount to a restriction on propositional justification which isn't far from denying [CPJ]. So it is not out of character for the pragmatist to deny [CPJ] by adopting the modifications I've proposed in this Section.

Let's recap. In Chapter One I introduced the Argument from Evidential Circularity, and in Chapters Two and Three I've developed a response to it which trades on adopting a pragmatist theory of justified belief. But in Section 4.1 I showed that, unless

[27] There are also closure principles which concern your knowledge that the deductive entailment holds, in addition to its being true that it does. I've formulated [CPJ] without this extra component because I'm concerned with avoiding illegitimate propositional justification, which doesn't require knowing that he relevant entailments hold. However, closure principles with this extra provision will also fail on my account, as a result of my denial of [CPJ].

it is modified, the pragmatist theory licenses intuitively unappealing bootstrapping procedures. Although these aren't epistemically circular per se, they do detract from the plausibility of pragmatism as a response to the Argument from Evidential Circularity. So in this Section I've proposed a modification to the pragmatist theory, which involves placing normative constraints on your ability to pay attention to particular combinations of beliefs. This removes the possibility of gaining justification – even propositional justification – by bootstrapping for pragmatists.

Before I move on, I should note that there have been several proposed solutions to the Bootstrapping Problem by basic justification theorists. I won't comment on whether these proposals succeed, since I've focussed on developing an under-investigated line of response to evidential circularity. I've tried to show that we can avoid circularity even if we affirm [JR]. However, what I've said about bootstrapping for pragmatists might be relevant to the problem of bootstrapping for basic justification theorists.[28] As I've said, a fully detailed version of my proposal would have to say a lot more about placing normative justificatory constraints on attention, and it may turn out that these can help us avoid ordinary cases of bootstrapping as well. So what I've said has implications beyond the problem at hand.

[28] Notice that the inference to [22] in the Argument from Evidential Circularity seems to require closure. So one response currently under debate is to deny that closure applies in ordinary bootstrapping cases. See Becker (2012, 2013), Bondy (2014) and Lockard (2014) for discussion.

Chapter Five: The Argument from Theoretic Circularity

In Chapter One I discussed an argument for thinking that epistemically circular justification is possible which focuses on our evidential sources. I have called it the Argument from Evidential Circularity. This argument is the central problem in debates over epistemic circularity, but I have tried to show that it is not decisive. My response involves affirming [JR] with respect to our evidential sources, but denying that you can only justify their reliability by evidence. Instead, I have defended the pragmatist view that you can justify a source's reliability by appealing your goals and preferences. My response draws on an argument offered by Byeong Lee (2014), but makes substantial modifications to his account.

In this Chapter I will present an entirely new argument for thinking that epistemically circular justification is possible. Whilst the Argument from Evidential Circularity focussed on our evidential sources, the new argument will focus on our theories of justification. Accordingly, we can call it the Argument from Theoretic Circularity. My view is that the Argument from Theoretic Circularity is much more convincing than the Argument from Evidential Circularity. So I conclude that epistemically circular justification is possible, but not for the reasons that have typically been thought.

I will formulate my argument in Section 5.1. In Section 5.2, I will consider some possible responses to it, and argue that they don't succeed. Then, in Section 5.3, I will consider its implications – in particular, for the question of what distinguishes permissible instances of epistemic circularity from impermissible ones.

5.1 *Theoretic Circularity*

It is generally thought that some of our beliefs are justified. A major project in epistemology has been to analyse what makes them justified. Let us denote any proposed set of conditions for justification using the character 'δ'. Accordingly, we can say that any theory explaining what makes claims justified has the following basic form:

> [T]: δ is a justification source such that: for any claim P, P is justified IFF δ provides justification for P.

The content of δ will obviously vary depending on the details of the account at hand. For instance, if [T] is a process reliabilist theory, then δ will be a set of conditions specifying that P is caused or sustained by a reliable process. If [T] is a coherentist theory, then δ will be a set of properties describing P's coherence with the rest of your belief system. Likewise, if [T] is a foundationalist theory, then δ will be a set of disjunctive conditions such that P is either a foundational belief or supported by foundational beliefs. More examples could be provided, but whatever their details, the same basic form will hold. [T] identifies the ultimate set of conditions of justification.

Theories of form [T] are not so much analyses of what justification is, as they are analyses of how justification is ultimately provided. Of course, there might be room to debate whether there is much difference. My own view is that there isn't one. For instance, I think that a process reliabilist account which analyses justification in terms of reliable processes would be equally a definition of justification as it would be a theory of how justification is gained. But I'm willing to allow that some might not share my view, so I'll restrict myself to saying that theories of what provides justification (and not necessarily analyses of what justification is) have the form [T].

In order to inquire rationally into what justifies our beliefs, it is necessary to make some background assumptions. Firstly, we need to assume (at least from the outset) that it is possible to believe a theory of justification which is correct. If we don't assume this, it is hard to see what we could be doing when we inquire into what makes our beliefs justified. And when we come to believe any theory of justification, what we believe is that it is correct. So it would be irrational to pursue or defend a theory of justification without assuming that it is at least possible to believe a correct theory.

We also need to assume (at least from the outset) that the correct theory of justification can be justified. Debates about justification are conducted by proposing theories and arguing for them. They involve providing reasons for and against particular views, adducing examples and counterexamples, and appealing to theoretical virtues such as simplicity, intuitive plausibility and explanatory power. This is best explained as a process of trying to justify our theories over those of our interlocutors. If we didn't think our theories could ever be justified, we would have a very good reason not to believe them.

It would also be hard to see why we should care about justification in the first place if we didn't care about justifying our theories. When we inquire into justification, we don't generally inquire into the justification of only particular subsets of beliefs. We are interested in justification generally, and this means that our theories of justification should also capture facts about what justifies our theories. So we ought to believe that it's at least possible that the correct theory of justification is justified.

Accordingly, rational inquiry into what justifies our beliefs requires assuming:

There is a possible theory of form [T] which is both correct and justified.

It is easy to show that this entails the existence of epistemically circular justification. [T] affirms that any justified claim can only be justified by δ. Since [T] is true and justified, it is justified by δ. So δ justifies the claim that it is a source of justification. According to the definition I proposed in Section 1.1, this is an instance of epistemic circularity.

Here is the Argument from Theoretic Circularity formulated more clearly:

1. There is a possible theory of form [T] which is both correct and justified. [Premise]

2. If [T] is correct then (δ is a justification source such that: for any claim P, P is justified IFF δ provides justification for P). [Premise]

3. ∴ If [T] is correct then ([T] is justified IFF δ provides justification for [T]). [2]

4. ∴ It is possible that δ provides justification for [T]. [1, 3]

5. ∴ It is possible that δ provides justification for the claim 'δ is a justification source such that: for any claim P, P is justified IFF δ provides justification for P'. [4]

6. ∴ It is possible that δ provides justification for the claim 'δ is a justification source'. [5]

7. [EC-J]: An instance of epistemically circular justification is one in which a justification source S provides you with justification for the claim 'S is a justification source'. [Premise]

8. ∴ Epistemically circular justification is possible. [6, 7]

Premise [1] is the rational presupposition for inquiry into what justifies our beliefs. Premise [2] just states that that the content of [T] is true whenever [T] is true, and [3] is an instantiation from [2]. Since [1] affirms that [T] is possibly true and justified, and since [3] affirms that if it is true and justified, provides justification for [T], it follows that it's possible that δ provides justification for [T]. From there is its straightforward to infer that, given the definition of circularity I proposed in Section 1.1, epistemically circular justification is possible.

So we get a situation in which our theory of justification is justified on its own terms. The details will obviously vary depending upon the theory at hand, but the result is the same. For instance, if [T] is a foundationalist theory, then [T] itself can only be justified by being a foundational claim or supported by foundational claims. Similarly, if [T] is a process reliabilist theory, then [T] can only be justified in virtue of being caused or sustained by a reliable process. Notice that [T] isn't merely consistent with what it identifies as the source of justification. It's justified *in virtue of* that source. What else could a theory of justification appeal to? Since δ is meant to provide the ultimate set of conditions for justification, capturing the full story about where justification comes from, the result – whatever the details – is that the theory can only be justified on its own terms. And that makes its justification epistemically circular.

What about pragmatism? According to the pragmatist, your goals and preferences are sources of justification, but it is open to the pragmatist to maintain that other sources can sometimes provide justification as well (for instance, in Section 3.3 I defended the special evidential status of introspection despite using an otherwise pragmatic account). Their view is just that pragmatic considerations are part of the picture. So a pragmatic theory will still fit into formulation [T]: δ will still describe the ultimate sources of justification for that theory, and at least one of these sources will be pragmatic.

This means that it won't be possible to construct a pragmatic response to the Argument from Theoretic Circularity that is analogous to the one I developed for the Argument from Evidential Circularity. A true and justified pragmatist theory will end up being justified on its own terms: either by prudential considerations, or by whatever non-prudential considerations the theory includes in its conditions δ.

It's important to remember that epistemically circular justification doesn't have to be doxastic in nature: it can also be propositional. Propositional justification is the kind of justification you can have for a claim even if you don't yet believe it. As I pointed out in Section 1.1, there is no reason to restrict epistemic circularity to the justification of claims that are already believed. Epistemic circularity can affect justificatory structures, wherein a particular source provides you with propositional justification for the claim that it is a justification source. So the correct theory of justification can be justified in an epistemically circular manner, even if no one has come to believe the correct theory yet.

James Van Cleve (1979) and Shatz (1983) have raised similar concerns. They worry that foundationalism, if true and justified, could only be justified in virtue of being foundationally supported. My argument takes this thought further by showing that *any* analysis of what provides justification – foundationalist or not – will face epistemic circularity. I've also tried to provide a more rigorous explanation for why this is the case by showing how it follows from the structure of [T], and by proposing a definition of epistemic circularity.

Similarly, Michael Bergmann (2004) has argued that sensible foundationalists are committed to thinking that it is possible to have justified beliefs about the sources of justification which are supported in part by those sources. Again, my argument has an advantage over Bergmann's because it generalises this observation beyond foundationalism. I've formulated [T] in a way that will capture all explanations of what provides justification, and I've proposed a definition of what epistemically circular justification is.

Inquiry into what makes our beliefs justified is one of the central projects of epistemology. To engage in this project, we must assume (at least from the outset) that it is possible to believe a theory of justification which is both true and justified. This commits us to thinking that epistemically circular justification is possible, for a true and justified theory can only be justified on its own terms. So unless we agree that epistemically circular justification is possible, one of epistemology's most central projects is a doomed enterprise. All theories of justification are either false, unjustified, or circular.

5.2 Responses to Theoretic Circularity

How might we respond to the Argument from Theoretic Circularity? The simplest response is to accept that epistemically circular justification is possible. But this involves taking on the dialectical ineffectiveness problem and the bad company problem. That is, it would involve explaining why circular structures can provide justification even though they are dialectically ineffective, as well as explaining why some instances of self-verification provide justification and some do not. I'll say more about these problems in Section 5.3, but first I want to consider two ways of trying to avoid the conclusion that epistemically circular justification is possible.

The Argument from Theoretic Circularity has only three premises, but one of them is just the definition of circularity I'm working with, and another is just the trivial claim that the content of [T] is correct whenever [T] is correct. So the only real way to respond to the argument is to deny premise [1]: that there is a possible theory of form [T] which is both correct and justified.

The first way to deny this claim is reminiscent of a move I considered in Section 3.1. This involves distinguishing the fact that an epistemic principle is true from the fact that it is justified. Presumably, only the truth of the principle is necessary for justification to occur in accordance with it. For instance, if process reliabilism happens to be the correct theory of justification, then all that's needed for us to have justified beliefs is for them to be reliably caused or sustained. Having justification for thinking that they are shouldn't be an extra requirement. So the suggestion is that we don't have to assume that it's possible for our theories to be justified, as long as it's possible that they are true.

This weakens our epistemic ambitions considerably. As I noted in Section 3.1, if we are content with trusting to the fact that certain conditions provide justification, without also trying to determine whether they do, then we cannot ascribe more than conditional justification to our beliefs. That is, we can only say that 'our beliefs are justified *if* they meet conditions δ'. But that's an uninteresting claim. We might as well say that our beliefs are justified if they are justified. Giving up on having a justified theory of justification would mean giving up on really understanding what actually justifies our beliefs, not simply what would justify them if they were justified.

It would also mean giving up on closely related questions. For instance, we may be interested in which of our beliefs are justified and which are not, with a view towards improving our belief systems and our belief forming practices. There is evident utility in such inquiry, and it would seem that giving up on having justified beliefs about justification would seriously threaten our ability to pursue rationally this question.

Giving up on trying to have justified theories of justification would also seem to generate a bad company problem of its own. If it's permissible to have an unjustified theory of justification, then it would be permissible to hold any crazy theory without defending it. For instance, I might hold the view that for any claim P, P is justified if and only if I believe P on a Sunday. In order for me to have justified beliefs in accordance with this theory, it is only necessary that my wacky view be correct, and not necessary that it be justified. But we ought to care about having grounds to reject implausible theories as unjustified, so we ought not to ignore the demand for justifying claims about justification. To doubt that the correct theory of justification can be justified would be simply to trade one bad company problem for another.

Of course, theories of justification might be acceptable in virtue of instantiating other epistemically valuable properties besides justification. For instance, it may be that what we're after is knowledge about justification, rather than justified belief about justification. And on some views, properties like knowledge and justification can come apart, such that we can have knowledge without thereby having justified belief. So one suggestion might be that our theories of justification don't need to be justified: they are acceptable as long as they instantiate another epistemically valuable property instead.

This response only pushes the problem back a step. The Argument from Theoretic Circularity is formulated in terms of justification, but a precisely analogous problem applies to every other epistemically valuable property as well. In Section 1.1, when I formulated my definition of circular justification, I noted that this was an instance of a more general pattern. It is possible to talk about epistemically circular knowledge or warrant, for instance, just as it is possible to talk about epistemically circular justification, and the underlying structure is the same. This is captured by the following general definition. The character 'ε' refers to the property in question, whether this is justification, knowledge, warrant, rational acceptability, or something similar:

> [EC-ε]: An instance of epistemically circular ε is one in which an ε-source S provides you with ε for the claim 'S is an ε-source'.

Like justification, inquiry into the ultimate sources of knowledge and other epistemically valuable properties is a central project in epistemology. This inquiry is conducted by proposing theories of the following form:

> [Tε]: μ is an ε-source such that: for any claim P, P is ε IFF μ provides ε for P

Because the rational presuppositions for inquiry into ε will be the same as for inquiry into justification, any theory of ε which is true and which instantiates ε will be epistemically circular for the same reason as before. Any theory of ε which is true and which instantiates ε can only do so in virtue of what it identifies as the conditions by which ε is provided – which we can represent as μ. But then we have a situation wherein μ provides ε for the claim that it is a source of ε. So any theory of the form [Tε] which is both true and ε will be epistemically circular.

The form of this argument is equivalent to that of the previous one:

1. There is a possible theory of form [Tε] which is both correct and ε. [Premise]

2. If [Tε] is correct then (μ is an ε-source such that: for any claim P, P is ε IFF μ provides ε for P). [Premise]

3. ∴ If [Tε] is correct then ([Tε] is ε IFF μ provides ε for [Tε]). [2]

4. ∴ It is possible that μ provides ε for [Tε]. [1, 3]

5. ∴ It is possible that μ provides ε for the claim 'μ is an ε-source such that: for any claim P, P is ε IFF μ provides ε for P'. [4]

6. ∴ It is possible that μ provides ε for the claim 'μ is an ε-source'. [5]

7. [EC-ε]: An instance of epistemically circular ε is one in which an ε-source S provides you with ε for the claim 'S is an ε-source'. [Premise]

8. ∴ Epistemically circular ε is possible. [6, 7]

So the Argument from Theoretic Circularity that I formulated in Section 5.1 is only an instance of a more general pattern, whereby any analysis of an epistemically valuable property which is true and which instantiates that property instantiates it in a circular fashion. This means that epistemic circularity is a deep problem for epistemology. If it's ever possible to have a theory of knowledge, justification, warrant or rational acceptability which is true and which instantiates the property in question, then epistemically circular provision of that property is possible.

This makes it much more difficult to doubt that our theories of justification can be justified by maintaining that they can be acceptable in virtue of another property. To defend this line of response, you would need to accept that no correct analysis of an epistemically valuable property can ever instantiate that property, which is more difficult to maintain. It would be arbitrary to hold without explanation that circular knowledge or circular warrant is possible but that circular justification isn't. So denying the possibility of circular justification commits you to denying that the circular provision of any other epistemic property is possible as well, and hence to the implausible view that no correct epistemic analysis can ever instantiate what it analyses. Unless circular knowledge, or circular warrant, or circular rational acceptability is possible, the central projects of epistemology are doomed.

The problem is most acute if we consider what makes a claim rationally acceptable.[29] Let me stipulate that rationally acceptable claims are all and only those claims that you that you are permitted (in the most general, all-things-considered sense) to believe. (My own view is that rational acceptability and justification are the same thing, but some views allow that the two properties can come apart, so I won't insist on the point).

Take any theory which attempts to explain what makes claims rationally acceptable. Either the theory will be true or it won't be. If it's true, then either it will be rationally acceptable or it won't be. If it is true and rationally acceptable, then it can only be acceptable in virtue of what it identifies as the source of rational acceptability – so it will work out to be circular. As before, the result is that any theory of rational acceptability will be false, unacceptable, or circular.

Obviously, we don't want our theory of rational acceptability to be false. And we don't want a theory which is as unacceptable. And because rational acceptability is just the property of being such that you are permitted to accept a claim, it would be contradictory to say that our theory is rationally acceptable because it instantiates

[29] Thanks to Matthew O'Leary for suggesting this consideration.

another epistemically valuable property besides rational acceptability. So we ought to think that it's possible to have a theory of rational acceptability which is true and rationally acceptable, and hence that the provision of the property 'rational acceptability' can be circular.

Even if you are willing to give up on providing a theory of justification, you ought to think that it's possible to get a theory of rational acceptability. Surely, we ought to care about whether we rationally ought to believe what we do! But if you agree that it's possible to get an acceptable theory of rational acceptability, you are committed to thinking that epistemically circular provision of this property is possible. It would be arbitrary to hold that circularity is possible in the one case but not in the other.

So rejecting the assumption that the correct theory of justification can be justified is a hopeless response. The problem applies more broadly than to justification, so maintaining this line of response commits you to denying that *any* correct analysis of an epistemically valuable property can instantiate that property. This is a hard claim to maintain. Moreover, it would commit you to denying that an acceptable theory can ever be provided for what makes beliefs rationally acceptable. So it amounts to giving up on epistemology in a big way.

A second line of response to the Argument from Theoretic Circularity affirms that it's possible to have a correct and justified theory of justification, but denies that it's possible to have one of the same form as [T]. [T] identifies δ as the complete set of necessary and sufficient conditions for the provision of justification. So one suggestion is that, whilst we can identify some of the conditions for justification, we cannot (on pain of circularity) identify the full set. The idea is that the threat of circularity doesn't prevent our theories from being justified: it prevents them from being complete.

Although this restriction permits that our theories may be justified, it prevents us from being able to say for sure whether they are. This is because any correct identification of some sufficient conditions for justification could never be justified by those conditions. If it were justified by those conditions, then the conditions in question would justify the claim that they provide justification, which would be circular.

Consider, for instance, a reliabilist theory which identifies causation by a reliable process as a source of justification. If epistemic circularity is impossible, then the theory cannot be justified in virtue of being reliably caused. Since it identifies reliable causation as a source of justification, it must be justified by something other than reliable causation or it would be circular. So taking this line of response commits you to the view that whatever justifies theories of justification is necessarily unidentifiable.

I think this response fails also. For one thing, it looks *ad hoc*. There is little special reason, besides maintaining a ban on circularity, for thinking that there are conditions for justification which are necessarily unidentifiable. In addition, it would seem that (for the same reasons as before) the proponent of this view would also have to say the same about any epistemically valuable property. They would have to say, for example, that there are necessarily unidentifiable sources of knowledge and warrant as well. And that looks like a much more difficult view to maintain. It seems that there is no special reason, besides avoiding circularity, for thinking that the sources of our epistemically valuable properties are unidentifiable in principle.

This has methodological implications for epistemology. If it isn't possible for a theory to be justified except by necessarily unidentifiable conditions, then it isn't possible to reasonably debate which theory is more justified than another. And, since exactly the same result would apply to any other epistemically valuable property (for the same reasons as before), no epistemic theory could be rationally defended or challenged. Again, this would be most problematic for theories of rational acceptability, since we would be necessarily unable to access the conditions that make them acceptable. So again, this line of response seriously weakens our epistemic ambitions.

The only way to avoid the Argument from Theoretic Circularity is to deny that it's possible for a correct and complete theory of justification to be justified. I've argued that two main versions of this response fail, one of which denies that the correct theory of justification can be justified, and another of which denies that the correct theory of justification can be complete. I've tried to show that neither succeeds, mostly because the Argument from Theoretic Circularity reveals a general structural problem which affects any theory of an epistemically valuable property. So maintaining that epistemically circular justification is impossible by endorsing either of the responses I've considered will mean giving up on most of the central projects in epistemology.

I don't expect my objections to persuade anyone who is actually willing to give up on epistemology. I'm willing to concede that! What I've tried to show is that the theoretical costs of avoiding circularity (for someone who does wish to investigate rationally into justification and similar properties) are too high. This provides extra reason for accepting the Argument from Theoretic Circularity. As implausible as circular justification might have seemed at first, it is more plausible that circular justification exists than it is that our epistemic theories are necessarily unjustified or incomplete. So I conclude that epistemically circular justification is possible.

5.3 Permissible and Impermissible Circularity

The result that epistemically circular justification is possible might be surprising. As I noted in the Introduction, there are two intuitively appealing reasons for thinking that a source can never justify a claim affirming its own justificatory efficacy. Firstly, circular justifications are dialectically ineffective: if you already accept that a particular source provides justification, then there is no point in me trying to persuade you. And if you don't, then I won't be able to persuade you by relying on the source. Secondly, self-verifying sources keep bad company. All manner of dodgy sources, such as the gambler's fallacious reasoning or the testimony of a mystic guru, can purport to justify their own efficacy. And the fact that their justifications would be circular seems relevant to why they fail. So it would be preferable to disallow circular justification altogether.

Epistemologists who accept circularity have tried to explain away these problems. No one thinks that all instances of apparent circular justification are genuine (and that's not what the Argument from Theoretic Circularity shows either). So something needs to be said to distinguish permissible cases from impermissible ones, with a view towards also explaining how circular justification is possible despite being unpersuasive.

In this thesis I've focussed on the question of whether epistemically circular justification is possible. I've tried to show that the Argument from Evidential Circularity doesn't establish this, but that the Argument from Theoretic Circularity does. So I won't address the extra question of what distinguishes permissible from impermissible circularity in too much detail. However, I do think it would be helpful to mention an existing proposal, and to express my own views on how the question might be investigated further. Accordingly, treat this Section as mostly speculative.

One proposed distinction between permissible and impermissible circularity looks more closely at its apparent dialectical ineffectiveness. The reason circular arguments look unpersuasive is that it seems you either trust a particular a source or you don't, and either way there is a reason why an argument relying on that source should fail to persuade you. But things might not really be so simple. It may be the case that you trust the source in practice, but that you don't have an explicit belief to the effect that it is trustworthy. For instance, you might treat induction as reliable without having an explicit belief that it is. So the proposal is that circular arguments can justify sources whose trustworthiness is *implicitly* accepted, even if they cannot persuade you to accept a source which you explicitly accept or reject.

Versions of this proposal have been offered by Alston (1986), Bergmann (2004) and Schmitt (2004). Michael Bergmann's version relativises your acceptance or rejection of a source to your context. He claims:

> What we have [...] are two different contexts in which a belief in the trustworthiness of a belief source is formed. The first is a context in which the subject has doubt or is uncertain about the source's trustworthiness. As such, it is what I'll call a 'questioned source context'. In the second context, the subject has no such doubt or uncertainty so it isn't a questioned source context. In virtue of its not being a questioned source context it is what I'll call an 'unquestioned source context'. My proposal is that epistemic circularity in a questioned source context is malignant and that epistemic circularity in an unquestioned source context is benign. [Bergmann 2004, pp. 718-19]

I think Bergmann's proposal would benefit from distinguishing between two different uses to which we put the concept of justification. Sometimes when we seek to justify a belief, we are looking for a reason that would persuade someone to accept it. Traditionally, epistemologists have been interested in finding reasons that would be acceptable to radical sceptics. But a different motivation for being interested in justifying a belief is not to discover whether it is true, or to persuade someone that it is, but merely to explain *why* it is true. The idea is that the concept of justification has both a persuasive and an explanatory meaning. So I think Bergmann's proposal could be supplemented with the idea that circular justifications can explain *why* a source is trustworthy, even when they don't persuade someone *that* it is. The idea is that the explanatory role of justification is what's relevant in unquestioned source contexts, and the persuasive role is relevant in questioned ones.

Michael Dummett (1973b) has discussed this distinction with reference to epistemically circular justifications of deduction. It would seem that we cannot justify claims affirming the validity of our deductive inferential rules without ultimately relying on the rules themselves. But as Dummett points out:

> Our problem is not to persuade anyone, not even ourselves, to employ deductive arguments: it is to find a satisfactory explanation of the role of such arguments in our use of language. [...] Characteristically, in an explanation, the conclusion of the argument is given in advance; and it may well be that our only reason for believing the premises of the explanatory argument is that they provide the most plausible explanation for the truth of the conclusion. [Dummett 1973b: 1974, pg. 9]

What implications would these proposals have for our epistemic project? That depends on how we think about the nature of our inquiry. If we have serious doubts about our belief sources, then it seems we are interested in *whether* they provide justification. On the other hand, if we don't seriously doubt our sources, but only seek to explain our use of them, we are interested in explaining *why* they provide justification. I think that tackling the first project would require giving the kinds of reasons that would be acceptable to a sceptic, so that inquiry into whether our sources provide justification would take place in a questioned source context. Circular justification would be impermissible in that context.

It is for this reason that William Alston (1986) concluded that attaining 'full reflective justification' – that is, simultaneous justification for all of your belief sources – is impossible. His view is that although you can justify the efficacy of any particular source at a given time, epistemic circularity prevents you from being able to justify the efficacy of all your sources simultaneously. When you doubt them all at once, your justification evaporates:

> Thus the situation with respect to basic sources of belief is this. So far as epistemic circularity is concerned, I can justify, and be justified in, taking the source to be reliable and to be a source of justification. But as soon as I direct a critical scrutiny on this happy state of affairs it disappears before my eyes; it eludes my reflective grasp. [...] All is well so long as we rely on justification that obtains in fact and do not insist on demonstrating it. But as soon as we look back with a critical eye, we meet the fate of Orpheus.
> [Alston 1986, pg. 24]

On the other hand, if we are mostly concerned with explaining *why* our sources provide justification, rather than trying to work out whether they do, then it would seem that we are in an unquestioned source context in which circular justification is permissible. So if we accept something like Bergmann's proposal, the implications of circularity for our epistemic inquiries depend upon what we consider the object of those inquiries.

For my part, I am suspicious of Bergmann's account. His view would make it the case that doing epistemology is a way of losing justification rather than gaining it. That is, the more carefully we consider the efficacy of our justification sources, the closer we are to questions about whether they provide justification rather than simply about why they do, and hence we risk falling into contexts in which our justification is vitiated by circularity.

I've also tried to show that epistemic circularity is endemic to the justification of our theories themselves. When we attack or defend a particular theory of justification, it is surely the case that we are genuinely interested in *whether* it is justified and not simply in why it is. Epistemology is a contentious business, and the situation with respect to our theories of justification is more like one in which we seek to persuade our interlocutors than one in which we seek to explain a theory that everyone already accepts. If we care about having justified theories, then the consequence of the above proposal is that we better not debate justification at all!

Bergmann's distinction between questioned and unquestioned source contexts also does little towards mitigating the bad company problem. If circularity is permissible in unquestioned source contexts, then it's easy to imagine examples of dodgy self-verification that occur in such contexts. We can, for instance, imagine the mystical guru confidently proclaiming his own infallibility, or the clueless gambler confidently asserting that the gambler's fallacy is probably reliable, since it's never been before. Obviously we don't have to agree that *we* have justification to accept the efficacy of those sources. We are in a questioned source context with respect to the guru's testimony and the gambler's fallacy. But Bergmann's proposal allows that the guru and the gambler themselves have genuine justification. And even that conclusion should be disturbing. A distinction between permissible and impermissible circularity should give us more substantial grounds upon which to condemn obviously bogus instances of self-verification.

These objections might not be decisive – as I said, the content of this Section is mostly speculation on the implications of what I've said in the rest of this Chapter. However, I do think it's worth considering an alternative means by which to distinguish permissible from impermissible circularity. Don't take my suggestions as a fully-developed theory, but only as a possible direction for future inquiry.

I noted near the beginning of Section 5.1 that [T] is the general form for theories of justification. I was careful to mention that by this I meant theories of what provides justification, and not necessarily theories of what justification *is*. However, my own view is that there is actually no real difference. I think that a theory of what ultimately provides justification also tells us something about what the term 'justification' actually means. For instance, a process reliabilist theory which affirms that justification is ultimately provided by reliable processes would also make it the case that being caused or sustained by a reliable process is part of what's meant by the term 'justification' in the first place.

So justification for [T] is justification for an analytic claim which is meaning-constituting. We can compare this with the mystical guru's claim that his testimony provides justification. That doesn't look like an analytic claim. It doesn't look like a claim about the meaning of the term 'justification', but a claim about a state of the world. So I wonder whether we can say that genuine epistemically circular justification is possible for analytic claims about justification, but not for synthetic ones.

This proposal borrows from Boghossian's (2000, 2001) suggestion that deductive inferential rules can justify their own validity only if those rules are meaning-constituting (that is, only if the rules help to define the content of meaningful logical concepts in our language). My idea is to take this proposal concerning the justification of deduction (a problem I haven't looked at in this thesis) and to apply it to the justification of theories of justification.[30] I suggest that epistemic principles which constitute the meanings of properties like 'justification' can permissibly instantiate those properties in virtue of what they identify as the conditions for their instantiation. By contrast, epistemic claims which don't do anything towards fixing the meaning of the epistemic property in question cannot permissibly instantiate it in a circular fashion.

Of course, this only allows us to reject the guru's claim as justified if we assume that the guru actually is making a synthetic claim and not an analytic one. But it is easy to imagine a case in which the guru does intend the circular justification of his testimony to be meaning-constituting. That is, we can imagine a guru who pronounces his own testimony a source of justification, and who intends this claim to be partially constitutive of the term 'justification' itself.

[30] For discussion of circularity problems with respect to the justification of deduction, see Boghossian (2000, 2001), Dummett (1973b: 1974, 1991) and Haack (1976, 1982).

I think this actually changes the nature of the problem. Once the proponent of a dodgy justification source tries to justify it by changing the meaning of the term, it will no longer be clear that they are actually working with something we should recognise as the concept of justification at all. It would be their understanding of the concept that we really ought to question. So we are under no obligation to say that even the guru himself is justified in virtue of trying to alter the meaning of the term 'justification'. Although he uses the term 'justification', we would have legitimate grounds to wonder whether he is making meaningful use of the concept in the first place.

To motivate this suggestion further, consider the example of stipulation. 'Stipulation' can be a source of justification for claims of a certain kind (namely, definitional claims), because stipulation is what makes certain concepts meaningful. Provided you are in the right conditions to stipulate a claim, the result is that your stipulated claims are analytically true. When I stipulate, for instance, that 'all bachelors are unmarried males', the stipulative process which makes the term 'bachelor' mean what it does also makes the claim 'all bachelors are unmarried males' true. It is plausible that a successful stipulation can justify that kind of claim in virtue of this fact.

If stipulation does count as a justification source, then it is an excellent example of the kind of source that can legitimately justify its own efficacy in a circular fashion. I can *stipulate* that stipulation is a reliable means of coming to form true definitional beliefs. Stipulation is (by stipulation!) just *what makes* those beliefs true. So if a stipulative process can justify certain meaning-constituting claims, then it can justify a claim affirming its reliability with respect to those claims. This means that it can justify its own justificatory efficacy in a circular fashion. It is one example of a source which confers legitimate circular justification in virtue of being meaning-constituting.

I admit that my proposal is quite sketchy, and developing it properly would require going into a lot more detail (for instance, it would require some defence of the view that the distinction between analytic and synthetic claims is genuine). However, don't take what I've said as a fully worked out theory, but more as a suggestion for future inquiry. Given that I've established that circular justification is at least possible, and in view of the bad company problem and the dialectical ineffectiveness problem, something needs to be said to distinguish permissible cases of circularity from impermissible cases. I think that existing proposals (such as Bergmann's) fail to adequately address this question, so I've speculated a little about an alternative way of looking at it. Because I think epistemic circular justification is possible for epistemic theories but probably not for evidential sources, and because I think our theories are meaning-constituting, my suspicion is that the permissibility of certain epistemically circular justifications might have something to do with what fixes the meanings of our epistemic terms.

Conclusion

An instance of epistemically circular justification is one in which a justification source justifies the claim that it is a justification source. A similar general pattern can apply to other epistemically valuable properties like knowledge, warrant and rational acceptability, but for the purposes of this thesis, I have mainly focussed on epistemically circular justification.

Epistemically circular justification is generally considered impossible. For one thing, circular arguments are unpersuasive. For another, certain dodgy evidential sources and inferential rules purport to be self-justifying, and the fact that their justifications would be circular seems relevant to an explanation of why they fail.

In this thesis I have examined two arguments for thinking that epistemically circular justification is possible. I have called the first the Argument from Evidential Circularity. Although this argument (in various forms) is the main extant argument for thinking that circular justification is possible, I've tried to show that it is not decisive. Instead, I've proposed the Argument from Theoretic Circularity, which I think is much more convincing. So I conclude that epistemically circular justification is possible, but not for the reasons that have typically been thought.

The Argument from Evidential Circularity chiefly concerns the claim that, in order to gain justification from an evidential source, you need justification to think it reliable. I have called this principle [JR]. The argument tries to show that affirming and denying [JR] each commit you to the possibility of epistemic circularity, and consequently that it is possible whatever your theory of justification.

In Section 1.2, I showed that affirming [JR] presents you with a version of the ancient Problem of the Criterion. Because it would seem that you can only justify an evidential source's reliability by appealing to another evidential source, we face a justificatory regress. And because the number of our fundamental evidential sources is finite, the regress can only terminate with a source whose reliability is justified in an epistemically circular fashion.

In Section 1.3, I showed that denying [JR] presents you with the Bootstrapping Problem. If you can gain justification from a source without having justification for its reliability, then you can quickly put yourself in a position to justify its reliability anyway. This is because you can use the outputs of the source as inductive evidence for its tendency to produce true outputs. Again the result is an instance of epistemically circular justification.

Although proposed responses to the Argument from Evidential Circularity mainly focus on the Bootstrapping Problem, my project has been to investigate an under-examined line of response which focuses on the Problem of the Criterion. It involves denying that you can only justify a source's reliability by evidence, instead appealing to the relationship between our evidential sources and our epistemic goals. This means endorsing pragmatism about justification, the view that your goals and preferences can justify claims, even when you lack sufficient evidence for those claims. I explained and motivated this view in Section 2.1.

An existing pragmatic approach to evidential circularity has been developed by Byeong Lee (2014). I explained his argument in Section 2.2. Lee's view is that we should accept the reliability of our sources because they stand the best chance of helping us acquire true beliefs in such a manner as to also avoid acquiring false ones.

Of course, the argument will only work if this is a reasonable goal, and I argued in Section 2.3 that Lee's original justifications for it are too weak. Whilst it might be possible to trust simply to the fact that the goal is reasonable (whether or not we can justify the claim that it is), I argued in Section 3.1 that we should not ignore the demand for acquiring internally-accessible reasons to accept it.

My approach treats our epistemic goal as a preference that we tend to have, which is reasonable by default and which isn't generally incompatible with our other preferences. I explained this view, which is a broadly Humean view of preferences, in Section 3.2.

Of course, coming to know that we prefer what we do requires introspective access to our mental states, and introspection is amongst the sources Lee originally tries to justify. Relying on his argument would be to justify introspection in a circular fashion, which I've tried to avoid in my response to the Argument from Evidential Circularity. So in Section 3.3 I defended the view that we have a default entitlement to the claim that our introspective faculties are reliable which doesn't rely on a pragmatic justification. My proposal is that [JR] is true with respect to all of our evidential sources, and that its requirement is met automatically in the case of introspection and via a pragmatic argument in the case of our other evidential sources.

In Section 4.1, I presented a novel version of the Bootstrapping Problem for pragmatism. Although it doesn't commit pragmatists to the possibility of epistemically circular justification per se, it does detract from the plausibility of the pragmatist theory as a potential response to the Argument from Theoretic Circularity. So in Section 4.2 I proposed some modifications to the pragmatist theory, which involve placing certain restrictions on combining the content of prudential reasoning with prudentially justified beliefs.

So the Argument from Evidential Circularity isn't completely decisive. Instead, I think that we are committed to the possibility of epistemically circular justification for a different reason. In Section 5.1 I formulated a new argument, which I call the Argument from Theoretic Circularity. The idea is that rational inquiry into the ultimate sources of justification requires thinking that it's at least possible to have a correct and justified theory about those sources. But such a theory can only be justified in a circular fashion – it can only appeal to what it identifies as the source of justification. So rational inquiry into justification requires thinking that epistemically circular justification is possible.

In Section 5.2 I considered two responses to this argument, one of which denies that the correct theory of justification must be justified, and the other of which denies that the correct theory of justification must be complete. I tried to show that each response requires giving up on epistemology in a big way, because the Argument from Theoretic Circularity is just an instance of a more general problem affecting any epistemically valuable property. So unless properties like justification, knowledge, warrant and rational acceptability can be provided in a circular fashion, inquiry into any of these properties is a doomed enterprise.

This result might be surprising, in view of the fact that circular justifications are unpersuasive and the fact that circularity seems relevant to an explanation of why many obviously dodgy attempts at self-justification fail. So an explanation is needed of what distinguishes permissible (or genuine) instances of circularity from impermissible ones. Although this extra question hasn't been my main focus, I have briefly considered it in Section 5.3. My view is that existing accounts of the distinction are inadequate, and that the permissibility of certain instances of epistemic circularity may have something to do with what constitutes the meanings of our epistemic concepts. I hope to have established both an interesting result and a motivation for future inquiry.

Appendix A: Principles and Definitions

A.1 My Definitions of Epistemic Circularity

[EC-J]: An instance of epistemically circular justification is one in which a justification source S provides you with justification for the claim 'S is a justification source.'

[EC-ε]: For any epistemically valuable property ε, an instance of epistemically circular ε is one in which an ε-source S provides you with ε for the claim 'S is an ε-source.'

A.2 The [JR] Principle

[JR]: For any evidential source S, S provides you with justification only if you have justification for the claim 'S is reliable.'

[~JR]: There is an evidential source G such that G provides you with justification even when you lack justification for the claim 'G is reliable.'

A.3 Byeong Lee's Epistemic Goal

[T]o acquire correct information about the world in such a way that reduces the risk of getting incorrect information. [Lee 2014, pg. 5]

A.4 Beliefs with Perceptual Content and Beliefs about Perceptual Content

[H]: 'I have hands.'

[~JH]: 'I am not justified in believing 'I have hands.''

A.5 Optimism in the Face of Evidence

[3] 'I am prudentially justified in believing 'I will survive this illness.''

[3*] 'I am not evidentially justified in believing 'I will survive this illness.''

[4] 'I will survive this illness.'

[5] ''I will survive this illness' is correct.'

A.6 A Closure Principle for Propositional Justification

[CPJ]: If you have propositional justification for premises [p1-p*n*], and [p1-p*n*] deductively entail conclusion [Q], then you have propositional justification for [Q].

A.7 The Structure of an Epistemic Theory

[T]: δ is a justification source such that: for any claim P, P is justified IFF δ provides justification for P.

[Tε]: μ is an ε-source such that: for any claim P, P is ε IFF μ provides ε for P

Appendix B: Arguments

B.1 The Argument from Evidential Circularity

1. [JR]: For any evidential source S, S provides you with justification only if you have justification for the claim 'S is reliable'. [Assumed]

2. There is an evidential source S1 which provides you with justification. [Premise]

3. ∴ You have justification for the claim 'S^1 is reliable'. [1, 2]

4. For any evidential source S, justification for the claim 'S is reliable' can only come from an evidential source. [Premise]

5. For any evidential sources S^A, S^B and S^C, if your justification for the claim 'S^C is reliable' comes from S^B, and your justification for the claim 'S^B is reliable' comes from S^A, then your justification for the claim 'S^C is reliable' ultimately comes from S^A. [Premise]

6. You have only a finite number of evidential sources. [Premise]

7. ∴ There is a source S^N such that your justification for the claim 'S^1 is reliable' ultimately comes from S^N. [3, 4, 5, 6]

8. ∴ You have justification for the claim 'S^N is reliable'. [1, 7]

9. ∴ Either S^N provides you with justification for the claim 'S^N is reliable' directly, or a source whose reliability is supported by S^N provides you with justification for the claim 'S^N is reliable'. [4, 5, 6, 8]

10. ∴ If a source whose reliability is supported by S^N provides you with justification for the claim 'S^N is reliable', then S^N ultimately provides you with justification for the claim 'S^N is reliable'. [5]

11. ∴ S^N provides you with justification for the claim 'S^N is reliable'. [8, 9, 10]

12. If S^N provides you with justification for the claim 'S^N is reliable', then S^N provides you with justification for the claim 'S^N is a justification source'. [Premise]

13. ∴ S^N provides you with justification for the claim 'S^N is a justification source'. [11, 12]

14. [EC-J]: An instance of epistemically circular justification is one in which a justification source S provides you with justification for the claim 'S is a justification source'. [Premise]

15. ∴ If S^N provides you with justification for the claim 'S^N is a justification source', then epistemically circular justification is possible. [14]

16. ∴ Epistemically circular justification is possible. [13, 15]

17. ∴ If [JR] is correct, then epistemically circular justification is possible. [Suppositional reasoning from 1-16; Assumption 1 Discharged]

18. [~JR]: There is an evidential source G such that G provides you with justification even when you lack justification for the claim 'G is reliable'. [Assumed]

19. If [~JR] then G can provide you with justification for claims P^1 - P^N. [Premise]

20. $\therefore$ G can provide you with justification for claims P^1 - P^N. [18, 19]

21. Each of P^1 - P^N entails a claim affirming that it is correct. [Premise]

22. $\therefore$ G can provide you with justification for claims affirming that P^1 - P^N are all correct. [20, 21]

23. You have justification for claims affirming that P1 - PN are each outputs of G. [Premise]

24. $\therefore$ G can provide you with justification for claims affirming that G is correct about each of P^1 - P^N. [22, 23]

25. Claims affirming that G is correct about each of P^1 - P^N jointly inductively entail that 'G is reliable'. [Premise]

26. $\therefore$ G can provide you with justification for the claim 'G is reliable'. [24, 25]

27. If G provides you with justification for the claim 'G is reliable', then G provides you with justification for the claim 'G is a justification source'. [Premise]

28. $\therefore$ G can provide you with justification for the claim 'G is a justification source'. [26, 27]

29. [EC-J]: An instance of epistemically circular justification is one in which a justification source S provides you with justification for the claim 'S is a justification source'. [Premise]

30. ∴ If G can provide you with justification for the claim 'G is a justification source', then epistemically circular justification is possible. [29]

31. ∴ Epistemically circular justification is possible. [28, 30]

32. ∴ If [~JR] is correct, then epistemically circular justification is possible. [Suppositional reasoning from 18-31; Assumption 18 Discharged]

33. ∴ Epistemically circular justification is possible. [17, 32]

B.2 Roxanne's Bootstrapping Inference

i. According to my gauge, my tank is full at present. [Premise]

ii. My tank is full at present. [Premise]

iii. ∴ 'My tank is full at present' is correct. [ii]

iv. ∴ What my gauge says is correct on this occasion. [i, iii]

v. [conclusions derived from many more inferences of the form i-iv] [Premise]

vi. ∴ What my gauge says is always correct. [Induction from iv, v]

vii. ∴ My gauge is reliable. [vi]

[Adapted from Vogel, 2000, pp. 612-623]

B.3 Byeong Lee's Argument for Perception

1. It is reasonable for us to pursue the epistemic goal. [Premise]
2. The best means of bringing about the epistemic goal requires accepting the general reliability of our perceptual judgments. [Premise]
3. ∴ It is reasonable for us to accept the general reliability of our perceptual judgments. [1, 2]

[Lee 2014, pg. 10; adapted very slightly]

B.4 A Lee-Style Argument for Introspection

1. It is reasonable for us to pursue the epistemic goal. [Premise]
2. The best means of bringing about the epistemic goal requires accepting the general reliability of our introspective judgments. [Premise]
3. ∴ It is reasonable for us to accept the general reliability of our introspective judgments. [1, 2]

B.5 Bootstrapping for Pragmatists

1. I am prudentially justified in trying to survive this illness. [Premise]
2. The best means of bringing it about that I will survive this illness is to believe 'I will survive this illness'. [Premise]
3. ∴ I am prudentially justified in believing 'I will survive this illness'. [1, 2]
4. I will survive this illness. [Premise]
5. ∴ 'I will survive this illness' is correct. [4]
6. ∴ What I am prudentially justified in believing is correct (in this instance). [3, 5]
7. [conclusions derived from many more inferences of the form 1-6] [Premises]
8. ∴ Whenever I am prudentially justified in believing a claim, that claim is correct. [Induction from 6, 7]
9. My evidence for a claim is just whatever increases my epistemic likelihood that the claim is correct. [Premise]
10. ∴ My prudential reasoning is a source of evidence. [8, 9]

B.6 The Argument from Theoretic Circularity

1. There is a possible theory of form [T] which is both correct and justified. [Premise]

2. If [T] is correct then (δ is a justification source such that: for any claim P, P is justified IFF δ provides justification for P). [Premise]

3. ∴ If [T] is correct then ([T] is justified IFF δ provides justification for [T]). [2]

4. ∴ It is possible that δ provides justification for [T]. [1, 3]

5. ∴ It is possible that δ provides justification for the claim 'δ is a justification source such that: for any claim P, P is justified IFF δ provides justification for P'. [4]

6. ∴ It is possible that δ provides justification for the claim 'δ is a justification source'. [5]

7. [EC-J]: An instance of epistemically circular justification is one in which a justification source S provides you with justification for the claim 'S is a justification source'. [Premise]

8. ∴ Epistemically circular justification is possible. [6, 7]

B.7 *The Argument from ε-Theoretic Circularity*

1. There is a possible theory of form [Tε] which is both correct and ε. [Premise]

2. If [Tε] is correct then (μ is an ε-source such that: for any claim P, P is ε IFF μ provides ε for P). [Premise]

3. ∴ If [Tε] is correct then ([Tε] is ε IFF μ provides ε for [Tε]). [2]

4. ∴ It is possible that μ provides ε for [Tε]. [1, 3]

5. ∴ It is possible that μ provides ε for the claim 'μ is an ε-source such that: for any claim P, P is ε IFF μ provides ε for P'. [4]

6. ∴ It is possible that μ provides ε for the claim 'μ is an ε-source'. [5]

7. [EC-ε]: An instance of epistemically circular ε is one in which an ε-source S provides you with ε for the claim 'S is an ε-source'. [Premise]

8. ∴ Epistemically circular ε is possible. [6, 7]

Bibliography

Alexander, D. (2011). 'In Defense of Epistemic Circularity.' *Acta Analytica* 26:3. 223-241.

Alston, W. (1986). 'Epistemic Circularity' *Philosophy and Phenomenological Research* 47:1. 1-30

Alston, W. (1993). *The Reliability of Sense Perception*. Ithaca: Cornell University Press. 12-17; 138-140.

Alston, W. (2005). *Beyond "justification": Dimensions of Epistemic Evaluation.* Ithaca: Cornell University Press.

Barnett D. (2014). 'What's the Matter with Epistemic Circularity?' *Philosophical Studies*. 171:2. 177-205.

Becker, K. (2012). 'Basic Knowledge and Easy Understanding.' *Acta Analytica* 27:2. 145-161.

Becker, K. (2013). 'Why Reliabilism Does Not Permit Easy Knowledge.' *Synthese* 190:17. 3751–3775.

Bergmann, M. (2000). 'Externalism and Skepticism.' *The Philosophical Review* 109:2. 159-194.

Bergmann, M. (2004). 'Epistemic Circularity: Malignant and Benign.' *Philosophy and Phenomenological Research* 69:3. 709-727.

Boghossian, P. (2000). 'Knowledge of Logic.' in Boghossian, P. (ed.). *New Essays on the A Priori*. Oxford: Oxford University Press.

Boghossian, P. (2001). 'How are objective epistemic reasons possible?' *Philosophical Studies* 106:1. 1-40.

Bondy, P. (2014). 'Epistemic Circularity, Reliabilism, and Transmission Failure.' *Episteme* 11:3. 335-348.

BonJour, L. (1985). *The Structure of Empirical Knowledge*. Cambridge: Harvard University Press.

Brender, E. (2006). 'Smoking Cessation'. *Journal of the American Medical Association* 296:1. (Online) URL: < http://jama.jamanetwork.com/article.aspx?articleid=211016 > Accessed 30/10/14.

Chisholm, R. (1973). *The Problem of the Criterion*. Milwaukee, WI: Marquette University Press.

Cohen, S. (2002). 'Basic Knowledge and the Problem of Easy Knowledge.' *Philosophy and Phenomenological Research* 65:2. 309–29.

Cohen, S. (2005). 'Why Basic Knowledge is Easy Knowledge.' *Philosophy and Phenomenological Research* 70:2. 417–430.

Cohen, S. (2010). 'Bootstrapping, Defeasible Reasoning, and a priori Justification.' *Philosophical Perspectives* 24. 141–59.

DeRose, K. (1999). 'Contextualism: An Explanation and Defense.' *The Blackwell Guide to Epistemology*. Greco, J. & Sosa, E. (eds.) Malden, MA. pp. 185–203.

Dummett, M. (1973b). 'The Justification of Deduction.' in Dummett, M. (1978) *Truth and Other Enigmas.* London: Duckworth

Dummett, M. (1973b: 1974). 'The Justification of Deduction.' *Henriette Hertz Trust Annual Philosophical Lecture, 1973*. London: Oxford University Press.

Dummett, M. (1991). *The Logical Basis of Metaphysics*. Cambridge, Mass.: Harvard University Press.

Feldman, R. (2000). 'The Ethics of Belief.' *Philosophy and Phenomenological Research* 60:3. 691-695.

Foley, R. (1991). 'Evidence and Reasons for Belief.' *Analysis* 51:2. 98-102.

Fumerton, R. (1995). *Metaepistemology and Skepticism*. Lanham, MD: Rowman & Littlefield. 178-179.

Goldman, A. (1979). 'What Is Justified Belief?' in Pappas, G. (ed.). *Justification and Knowledge*. Dordrecht: Reidel.

Goldman, A. (2008). 'Immediate Justification and Process Reliabilism.' in Smith, Q. (ed.). *Epistemology: New Essays*. Oxford: Oxford University Press.

Haack, S. (1976). 'The Justification of Deduction.' *Mind* 85:337. 112-119.

Haack, S. (1982). 'Dummett's Justification of Deduction'. *Mind* 91:362. 216-239.

Haunsperger, D. & Kennedy, S. (2007). *The Edge of the Universe: Celebrating Ten Years of Math Horizons*. The Mathematical Association of America. 5.

Hookway C. (2000). 'Epistemic norms and theoretical deliberation.' In Dancy, J. (ed.) *Normativity*. Oxford: Blackwell Publishers Ltd. 60-77.

Huemer, M. (2001). *Skepticism and the Veil of Perception*. Lanham, MD: Rowman & Littlefield.

Huemer, M. (2007). 'Compassionate Phenomenal Conservatism'. *Philosophy and Phenomenological Research* 74:1. 30-55.

Hume, D. (1739-40:1978). Selby-Bigge, L. & Nidditch, P. (eds.) *Treatise of Human Nature*. Second Edition. Oxford, Clarendon Press.

James, W. (1896: 1962). 'The Will to Believe.' Perry, R. (ed.) *Essays on Faith and Morals*. NY: World Publishing Co. 32-62.

Kallestrup, J. (2012). 'Bootstrap and Rollback: Generalizing Epistemic Circularity'. *Synthese* 189. 395–413.

Kelly, T. (2002). 'The Rationality of Belief and Some Other Propositional Attitudes.' *Journal of Philosophical Research* 110. 163-196.

Lee, B. (2014). 'Epistemic Principles and Epistemic Circularity.' *Philosophia*. 42:2. 413-432.

Lockard, M. (2014). 'Closure Provides No Relief from the Problem of Easy Knowledge.' *Erkenntnis* 79. 461-469.

Marušić, B. (2011). 'Ethics of Belief'. *Philosophy Compass* 6:1. 33-43.

Marušić, B. (2012). 'Belief and Difficult Action'. *Philosopher's Imprint* 12:18. 1-30.

Marušić, B. (2013). 'Promising Against the Evidence'. *Ethics* 123:2. 292-317.

Pascal, B. (1670:1978). *The Thoughts of Blaise Pascal*. Westport, Conn.: Greenwood Press.

Pryor, J. (2000). 'The Skeptic and the Dogmatist'. *Noûs* 34:4. 517-549.

Reed, B. (2006). 'Epistemic Circularity Squared? Scepticism about Common Sense.' *Philosophy and Phenomenological Research* 73:1. 186-197.

Reisner, A. (2008). 'Weighing Pragmatic and Evidential Reasons for Belief.' *Philosophical Studies* 138:1. 17-27.

Reisner, A. (2009). 'The Possibility of Pragmatic Reasons for Belief and the Wrong Kind of Reasons Problem.' *Philosophical Studies* 145:2. 257-272

Rosen, M. (2009). 'A Pragmatic Justification of Deduction' *Kritike* 3:1. 155-167

Schmitt, F. (2004). 'What is Wrong with Epistemic Circularity?' *Philosophical Issues* 14. 379-402.

Schwitzgebel, E. (2011a). 'Knowing your own beliefs.' *Canadian Journal of Philosophy*, 35, supplement 41–62. Hunter, D. (ed.) *Belief and Agency*,

Schwitzgebel, E. (2011b). *Perplexities of Consciousness*, Cambridge, MA: MIT.

Sellars, W. (1974b). 'Are there Non-Deductive Logics?' in Sellars, W. *Essays in Philosophy and its History*. Dordrecht: Reidel. pp. 437-38

Sextus Empiricus. *Outlines of Pyrrhonism*. Trans. Bury, R. (1990) Buffalo, N.Y.: Prometheus Books. 2:85.

Shatz, D. (1983). 'Foundationalism, Coherentism, and the Levels Gambit'. *Synthese* 55. 97-118.

Stroud, B. (1989). 'Understanding Human Knowledge in General.' In *Knowledge and Skepticism*. Clay, M. & Lehrer, K. (eds). Boulder: Westview Press. 31-49

Van Cleve, J. (1979). 'Foundationalism, Epistemic Principles, and the Cartesian Circle.' *The Philosophical Review* 88. 55–91.

Van Cleve, J. (2003). 'Is Knowledge Easy—or Impossible? Externalism as the Only Alternative to Skepticism.' In Luper, S. (ed.) (2003b). *The Sceptics*. Aldershot: Ashgate. 45–60.

Vogel, J. (2000). 'Reliabilism Leveled.' *Journal of Philosophy* 97:11. 602–23.

Weisberg, J. (2010). 'Bootstrapping in General.' *Philosophy and Phenomenological Research* 81:3. 525–48.

Williams, B. (1973). 'Deciding to believe.' In *Problems of the Self*. Cambridge: Cambridge University Press. 136-151

Zalabardo, J. (2005). 'Externalism, Skepticism, and the Problem of Easy Knowledge.' *The Philosophical Review* 114:1. 33-61.

CPSIA information can be obtained
at www.ICGtesting.com
Printed in the USA
LVHW032009220323
742311LV00014B/1197

9 781805 243779